AP-4A   ADVANCED PLACEMENT TEST SERIES

This is your
PASSBOOK for...

Computer Science A

Test Preparation Study Guide
Questions & Answers

COPYRIGHT NOTICE

This book is SOLELY intended for, is sold ONLY to, and its use is RESTRICTED to individual, bona fide applicants or candidates who qualify by virtue of having seriously filed applications for appropriate license, certificate, professional and/or promotional advancement, higher school matriculation, scholarship, or other legitimate requirements of education and/or governmental authorities.

This book is NOT intended for use, class instruction, tutoring, training, duplication, copying, reprinting, excerption, or adaptation, etc., by:

1) Other publishers
2) Proprietors and/or Instructors of "Coaching" and/or Preparatory Courses
3) Personnel and/or Training Divisions of commercial, industrial, and governmental organizations
4) Schools, colleges, or universities and/or their departments and staffs, including teachers and other personnel
5) Testing Agencies or Bureaus
6) Study groups which seek by the purchase of a single volume to copy and/or duplicate and/or adapt this material for use by the group as a whole without having purchased individual volumes for each of the members of the group
7) Et al.

Such persons would be in violation of appropriate Federal and State statutes.

PROVISION OF LICENSING AGREEMENTS – Recognized educational, commercial, industrial, and governmental institutions and organizations, and others legitimately engaged in educational pursuits, including training, testing, and measurement activities, may address request for a licensing agreement to the copyright owners, who will determine whether, and under what conditions, including fees and charges, the materials in this book may be used them. In other words, a licensing facility exists for the legitimate use of the material in this book on other than an individual basis. However, it is asseverated and affirmed here that the material in this book CANNOT be used without the receipt of the express permission of such a licensing agreement from the Publishers. Inquiries re licensing should be addressed to the company, attention rights and permissions department.

All rights reserved, including the right of reproduction in whole or in part, in any form or by any means, electronic or mechanical, including photocopying, recording, or by any information storage and retrieval system, without permission in writing from the Publisher.

Copyright © 2025 by
National Learning Corporation

212 Michael Drive, Syosset, NY 11791
(516) 921-8888 • www.passbooks.com
E-mail: info@passbooks.com

PASSBOOK® SERIES

THE *PASSBOOK® SERIES* has been created to prepare applicants and candidates for the ultimate academic battlefield – the examination room.

At some time in our lives, each and every one of us may be required to take an examination – for validation, matriculation, admission, qualification, registration, certification, or licensure.

Based on the assumption that every applicant or candidate has met the basic formal educational standards, has taken the required number of courses, and read the necessary texts, the *PASSBOOK® SERIES* furnishes the one special preparation which may assure passing with confidence, instead of failing with insecurity. Examination questions – together with answers – are furnished as the basic vehicle for study so that the mysteries of the examination and its compounding difficulties may be eliminated or diminished by a sure method.

This book is meant to help you pass your examination provided that you qualify and are serious in your objective.

The entire field is reviewed through the huge store of content information which is succinctly presented through a provocative and challenging approach – the question-and-answer method.

A climate of success is established by furnishing the correct answers at the end of each test.

You soon learn to recognize types of questions, forms of questions, and patterns of questioning. You may even begin to anticipate expected outcomes.

You perceive that many questions are repeated or adapted so that you can gain acute insights, which may enable you to score many sure points.

You learn how to confront new questions, or types of questions, and to attack them confidently and work out the correct answers.

You note objectives and emphases, and recognize pitfalls and dangers, so that you may make positive educational adjustments.

Moreover, you are kept fully informed in relation to new concepts, methods, practices, and directions in the field.

You discover that you are actually taking the examination all the time: you are preparing for the examination by "taking" an examination, not by reading extraneous and/or supererogatory textbooks.

In short, this PASSBOOK®, used directedly, should be an important factor in helping you to pass your test.

ADVANCED PLACEMENT PROGRAM

INTRODUCTION

The Advanced Placement Program is more than 50 years old, and since its creation by the College Board in 1955 it has offered more than 7 million examinations to more than 5 million candidates around the world. These candidates are usually high school juniors or seniors who have taken an AP or equivalent college-level course while still in secondary school.

Students participate in the AP Program for several reasons. Some enjoy the opportunity to be challenged by a college-level course while still in high school. Others appreciate the chance to be exempt from an introductory course once in college. Whatever the reason, participation in the AP Program provides an academically stimulating situation; it can also save a student money and time in college.

The validity and reliability of the AP Program are widely acknowledged. AP grades are now recognized by most two- and four-year colleges and universities both inside and outside of the United States. These institutions offer advanced placement, course credit, or both to students who have successfully completed AP Exams. In addition, many of these institutions grant sophomore standing to students who have demonstrated their competence in three or more exams.

The AP Program is more than just examinations, however. It also actively promotes college-level instruction at the high school level, specifically in the form of AP courses, faculty workshops, and facilitating publications. The College Board periodically monitors college-level courses throughout the nation to ensure that AP courses reflect the best college instruction. Every summer the Board holds workshops for AP teachers from the more than 10,000 high schools that offer AP courses and examinations. In addition, the Board has made available almost 300 publications containing information and data about the Program's products and services.

The Advanced Placement Program aims to improve the nation's quality of education and to facilitate students' transition from secondary school to college. Through its committees of educators, the AP Program provides course descriptions and examinations in 20 disciplines so that secondary schools may offer their students the stimulating challenge of college-level study culminating in an exam that measures college-level achievement.

At least two years are generally needed to develop each Advanced Placement Examination. The high school and college teachers on the development committee devise test questions that are subjected to repeated testing, review and revision. They evaluate each question and exam to eliminate any language, symbols, or content that may be offensive to or inappropriate for major subgroups of the test-taking population; statistical procedures help identify possibly unfair items. The questions that remain are assembled according to test specifications and, after further editing and checking, compose the AP Examination.

Every May, typically after a full academic year of advanced instruction, hundreds of thousands of students from almost one-half of the approximately 21,000 secondary schools in this country take one or more of the 35 AP Examinations offered. In all subjects except Studio Art, the exams contain both multiple-choice questions and free-response questions, the latter requiring essay writing and problem solving.

Grading AP Examinations is a unique enterprise: the size and complexity of the reading are on a scale unlike any other essay assessment in this country; the evaluation requires special and demanding procedures designed to produce equitable and consistent evaluations of performance. While the multiple-choice sections of the exams are scored by machine, the free-response sections require the involvement of thousands of college professors and AP teachers who have been carefully selected on the basis of their education, experience and association with the AP Program. Several hundred thousand examinations contain more than 3 million student answers. Several hundred individuals provide professional and clerical support. Three or more sites are required to accommodate the six-day reading.

While pride in accomplishing this huge task is justifiable, the essential concern of the Advanced Placement Program is that all students receive grades that demonstrate their achievement fairly and accurately. Thus, the following procedures are used to assure that grading standards are applied fairly to all papers:

- The conscientious development of scoring standards. The preparation of standards for an examination begins when the development committee reviews and approves the examination, which may be as much as two years before the reading. After the exam has been administered, the standards are refined by instructors who have experience working with actual candidate answers.

- The use of carefully developed scoring scales. Each question has an associated scoring scale designed to allow faculty consultants to make distinctions among answers. The scales — usually from 0 to 5, or 0 to 9 — avoid the problem of too few points, which allows only coarse distinctions, and the problem of too many points, which requires overly refined, often meaningless discriminations. Because the standards and their accompanying scales are tailored to individual questions, they allow each answer to be appropriately ranked.

- The rigorous review of the scoring standards and their internalization by all AP faculty consultants. Three to seven hours of the six-day reading period are devoted to reviewing the standards and making sure that they are applied consistently. The objective is to meld two essential components: (1) each faculty consultant's professional assessment of the answers, and (2) the scoring standards developed by the reading group. In this way, an accurate and uniform assessment of the papers is achieved.

- Minimization of the possibility of the *halo effect*. The *halo effect* (giving an answer a higher or lower grade than it deserves because of good or poor impressions of other answers by the same student) is minimized by following three practices: (1) having each question, or question set, read by a different faculty consultant; (2) completely masking all scores given by other faculty consultants; and (3) covering the candidate's identification information. These practices permit each faculty consultant to evaluate essay answers without being prejudiced by knowledge about the candidates. Having up to eight faculty consultants assess different questions within a given exam ensures that each answer is judged solely on its own merit.

- The close monitoring of scoring standards. Scoring standards are developed and monitored using a variety of methods that minimize the chances that students would receive different grades if their answers were read by different faculty consultants. One method is to have a second faculty consultant independently score exams that have been previously read; another method is to have the faculty consultant reread exams that he or she has previously read. In either instance, if there is too great a disparity between the resulting scores, the individuals involved resolve the differences. These are just two of the methods used to maintain the scoring standards. Taken as a whole, the procedures ensure that each candidate receives an accurate estimate of her or his demonstrated achievement on the AP Examination.

Examination Standards

Multiple-choice questions have the unique ability to cover the breadth of a curriculum. They have three other strengths: high reliability, controlled level of difficulty, and the possibility of establishing comparability with earlier examinations. Reliability, or the likelihood that candidates taking different forms of the examination will receive the same scores, is controlled more effectively with multiple-choice questions than with free-response questions.

Maintaining a specified distribution of questions at appropriate levels of difficulty ensures that the measurement of differences in students' achievement is optimized. For AP Examinations, the most important distinctions among students are between the grades of 2 and 3, and 3 and 4. These distinctions are usually best accomplished by using many questions of medium difficulty.

Comparability of scores on the multiple-choice section of a current and a previous examination is provided by incorporating a given number of items from an earlier examination within the current one, thereby allowing comparisons to be made between the scores of the earlier group of candidates and the current group. This information is used, along with other data, by the chief faculty consultant to establish AP grades that reflect the competence demanded by the Advanced Placement Program and that compare with earlier grades.

Student Preparation

This book, Rudman's Questions and Answers on the AP Examination, is highly recommended by the editors, educators and students to prepare for the multiple-choice part of the AP Examination as an immediate last step before taking the actual examination. Good luck!

AP COMPUTER SCIENCE

TOPIC OUTLINE

Following is an outline of the major topics considered for the AP Computer Science A Exam. This outline is intended to define the scope of the course, but not the sequence.

I. Object-Oriented Program Design

The overall goal for designing a piece of software (a computer program) is to correctly solve the given problem. At the same time, this goal should encompass specifying and designing a program that is understandable, and can be adapted to changing circumstances. The design process needs to be based on a thorough understanding of the problem to be solved

A. Program and Class Design
   1. Problem analysis
   2. Data abstraction and encapsulation
   3. Class specifications, interface specifications, relationships ("is-a," "has-a"), and extension using inheritance
   4. Code reuse
   5. Data representation and algorithms
   6. Functional decomposition

II. Program Implementation

Part of the problem-solving process is the statement of solutions in a precise form that invites review and analysis. The implementation of solutions in the Java programming language reinforces concepts, allows potential solutions to be tested, and encourages discussion of solutions and alternatives.

A. Implementation techniques
   1. Top-down
   2. Bottom-up
   3. Object-oriented
   4. Encapsulation and information hiding
   5. Procedural abstraction
B. Programming constructs
   1. Primitive types vs. reference types
   2. Declaration
      a. Constants
      b. Variables
      c. Methods and parameters
      d. Classes
      e. Interfaces
   3. Text output using System. out .print and System. out .println
   4. Control
      a. Method call
      b. Sequential execution
      c. Conditional execution
      d. Iteration
      e. Recursion

5. Expression evaluation
   a. Numeric expressions
   b. String expressions
   c. Boolean expressions, short-circuit evaluation, De Morgan's law
C. Java library classes and interfaces included in the AP Java Subset

III. Program Analysis

The analysis of programs includes examining and testing programs to determine whether they correctly meet their specifications. It also includes the analysis of programs or algorithms in order to understand their time and space requirements when applied to different data sets.

A. Testing
   1. Development of appropriate test cases, including boundary cases
   2. Unit testing
   3. Integration testing
B. Debugging
   1. Error categories: compile-time, run-time, logic
   2. Error identification and correction
   3. Techniques such as using a debugger, adding extra output statements, or hand-tracing code.
C. Runtime exceptions
D. Program correctness
   1. Pre- and post-conditions
   2. Assertions
E. Algorithm Analysis
   1. Statement execution counts
   2. Informal running time comparison
E Numerical representations of integers
   1. Representations of non-negative integers in different bases
   2. Implications of finite integer bounds

IV. Standard Data Structures

Data structures are used to represent information within a program. Abstraction is an important theme in the development and application of data structures.

A. Primitive data types (int, boolean, double)
B. Strings
C. Classes
D. Lists
E. Arrays (1-dimensional and 2-dimensional)

V. Standard Operations and Algorithms

Standard algorithms serve as examples of good solutions to standard problems. Many are intertwined with standard data structures. These algorithms provide examples for analysis of program efficiency.

A. Operations on data structures
   1. Traversals
   2. Insertions
   3. Deletions
B. Searching
   1. Sequential
   2. Binary
C. Sorting
   1. Selection
   2. Insertion
   3. Mergesort

VI. Computing in Context

An awareness of the ethical and social implications of computing systems is necessary for the study of computer science. These topics need not be covered in detail, but should be considered throughout the course.

A. System reliability
B. Privacy
C. Legal issues and intellectual property
D. Social and ethical ramifications of computer use

HOW TO TAKE A TEST

You have studied long, hard and conscientiously.

With your official admission card in hand, and your heart pounding, you have been admitted to the examination room.

You note that there are several hundred other applicants in the examination room waiting to take the same test.

They all appear to be equally well prepared.

You know that nothing but your best effort will suffice. The "moment of truth" is at hand: you now have to demonstrate objectively, in writing, your knowledge of content and your understanding of subject matter.

You are fighting the most important battle of your life—to pass and/or score high on an examination which will determine your career and provide the economic basis for your livelihood.

What extra, special things should you know and should you do in taking the examination?

I. YOU MUST PASS AN EXAMINATION

A. WHAT EVERY CANDIDATE SHOULD KNOW
Examination applicants often ask us for help in preparing for the written test. What can I study in advance? What kinds of questions will be asked? How will the test be given? How will the papers be graded?

B. HOW ARE EXAMS DEVELOPED?
Examinations are carefully written by trained technicians who are specialists in the field known as "psychological measurement," in consultation with recognized authorities in the field of work that the test will cover. These experts recommend the subject matter areas or skills to be tested; only those knowledges or skills important to your success on the job are included. The most reliable books and source materials available are used as references. Together, the experts and technicians judge the difficulty level of the questions.
Test technicians know how to phrase questions so that the problem is clearly stated. Their ethics do not permit "trick" or "catch" questions. Questions may have been tried out on sample groups, or subjected to statistical analysis, to determine their usefulness.
Written tests are often used in combination with performance tests, ratings of training and experience, and oral interviews. All of these measures combine to form the best-known means of finding the right person for the right job.

II. HOW TO PASS THE WRITTEN TEST

A. BASIC STEPS

1) Study the announcement

How, then, can you know what subjects to study? Our best answer is: "Learn as much as possible about the class of positions for which you've applied." The exam will test the knowledge, skills and abilities needed to do the work.

Your most valuable source of information about the position you want is the official exam announcement. This announcement lists the training and experience qualifications. Check these standards and apply only if you come reasonably close to meeting them. Many jurisdictions preview the written test in the exam announcement by including a section called "Knowledge and Abilities Required," "Scope of the Examination," or some similar heading. Here you will find out specifically what fields will be tested.

2) Choose appropriate study materials

If the position for which you are applying is technical or advanced, you will read more advanced, specialized material. If you are already familiar with the basic principles of your field, elementary textbooks would waste your time. Concentrate on advanced textbooks and technical periodicals. Think through the concepts and review difficult problems in your field.

These are all general sources. You can get more ideas on your own initiative, following these leads. For example, training manuals and publications of the government agency which employs workers in your field can be useful, particularly for technical and professional positions. A letter or visit to the government department involved may result in more specific study suggestions, and certainly will provide you with a more definite idea of the exact nature of the position you are seeking.

3) Study this book!

III. KINDS OF TESTS

Tests are used for purposes other than measuring knowledge and ability to perform specified duties. For some positions, it is equally important to test ability to make adjustments to new situations or to profit from training. In others, basic mental abilities not dependent on information are essential. Questions which test these things may not appear as pertinent to the duties of the position as those which test for knowledge and information. Yet they are often highly important parts of a fair examination. For very general questions, it is almost impossible to help you direct your study efforts. What we can do is to point out some of the more common of these general abilities needed in public service positions and describe some typical questions.

1) General information

Broad, general information has been found useful for predicting job success in some kinds of work. This is tested in a variety of ways, from vocabulary lists to questions about current events. Basic background in some field of work, such as sociology or economics, may be sampled in a group of questions. Often these are principles which have become familiar to most persons through exposure rather than through formal training. It is difficult to advise you how to study for these questions; being alert to the world around you is our best suggestion.

2) Verbal ability
An example of an ability needed in many positions is verbal or language ability. Verbal ability is, in brief, the ability to use and understand words. Vocabulary and grammar tests are typical measures of this ability. Reading comprehension or paragraph interpretation questions are common in many kinds of civil service tests. You are given a paragraph of written material and asked to find its central meaning.

IV. KINDS OF QUESTIONS

1. Multiple-choice Questions
Most popular of the short-answer questions is the "multiple choice" or "best answer" question. It can be used, for example, to test for factual knowledge, ability to solve problems or judgment in meeting situations found at work.
A multiple-choice question is normally one of three types:
- It can begin with an incomplete statement followed by several possible endings. You are to find the one ending which best completes the statement, although some of the others may not be entirely wrong.
- It can also be a complete statement in the form of a question which is answered by choosing one of the statements listed.
- It can be in the form of a problem – again you select the best answer.

Here is an example of a multiple-choice question with a discussion which should give you some clues as to the method for choosing the right answer:

When an employee has a complaint about his assignment, the action which will best help him overcome his difficulty is to
  A. discuss his difficulty with his coworkers
  B. take the problem to the head of the organization
  C. take the problem to the person who gave him the assignment
  D. say nothing to anyone about his complaint

In answering this question, you should study each of the choices to find which is best. Consider choice "A" – Certainly an employee may discuss his complaint with fellow employees, but no change or improvement can result, and the complaint remains unresolved. Choice "B" is a poor choice since the head of the organization probably does not know what assignment you have been given, and taking your problem to him is known as "going over the head" of the supervisor. The supervisor, or person who made the assignment, is the person who can clarify it or correct any injustice. Choice "C" is, therefore, correct. To say nothing, as in choice "D," is unwise. Supervisors have and interest in knowing the problems employees are facing, and the employee is seeking a solution to his problem.

2. True/False

3. Matching Questions
Matching an answer from a column of choices within another column.

V. RECORDING YOUR ANSWERS

Computer terminals are used more and more today for many different kinds of exams.

For an examination with very few applicants, you may be told to record your answers in the test booklet itself. Separate answer sheets are much more common. If this separate answer sheet is to be scored by machine – and this is often the case – it is highly important that you mark your answers correctly in order to get credit.

VI. BEFORE THE TEST

YOUR PHYSICAL CONDITION IS IMPORTANT

If you are not well, you can't do your best work on tests. If you are half asleep, you can't do your best either. Here are some tips:

1) Get about the same amount of sleep you usually get. Don't stay up all night before the test, either partying or worrying—DON'T DO IT!
2) If you wear glasses, be sure to wear them when you go to take the test. This goes for hearing aids, too.
3) If you have any physical problems that may keep you from doing your best, be sure to tell the person giving the test. If you are sick or in poor health, you relay cannot do your best on any test. You can always come back and take the test some other time.

Common sense will help you find procedures to follow to get ready for an examination. Too many of us, however, overlook these sensible measures. Indeed, nervousness and fatigue have been found to be the most serious reasons why applicants fail to do their best on civil service tests. Here is a list of reminders:

- Begin your preparation early – Don't wait until the last minute to go scurrying around for books and materials or to find out what the position is all about.
- Prepare continuously – An hour a night for a week is better than an all-night cram session. This has been definitely established. What is more, a night a week for a month will return better dividends than crowding your study into a shorter period of time.
- Locate the place of the exam – You have been sent a notice telling you when and where to report for the examination. If the location is in a different town or otherwise unfamiliar to you, it would be well to inquire the best route and learn something about the building.
- Relax the night before the test – Allow your mind to rest. Do not study at all that night. Plan some mild recreation or diversion; then go to bed early and get a good night's sleep.
- Get up early enough to make a leisurely trip to the place for the test – This way unforeseen events, traffic snarls, unfamiliar buildings, etc. will not upset you.
- Dress comfortably – A written test is not a fashion show. You will be known by number and not by name, so wear something comfortable.
- Leave excess paraphernalia at home – Shopping bags and odd bundles will get in your way. You need bring only the items mentioned in the official notice you received; usually everything you need is provided. Do not bring reference books to the exam. They will only confuse those last minutes and be taken away from you when in the test room.

- Arrive somewhat ahead of time – If because of transportation schedules you must get there very early, bring a newspaper or magazine to take your mind off yourself while waiting.
- Locate the examination room – When you have found the proper room, you will be directed to the seat or part of the room where you will sit. Sometimes you are given a sheet of instructions to read while you are waiting. Do not fill out any forms until you are told to do so; just read them and be prepared.
- Relax and prepare to listen to the instructions
- If you have any physical problem that may keep you from doing your best, be sure to tell the test administrator. If you are sick or in poor health, you really cannot do your best on the exam. You can come back and take the test some other time.

VII. AT THE TEST

The day of the test is here and you have the test booklet in your hand. The temptation to get going is very strong. Caution! There is more to success than knowing the right answers. You must know how to identify your papers and understand variations in the type of short-answer question used in this particular examination. Follow these suggestions for maximum results from your efforts:

1) Cooperate with the monitor

The test administrator has a duty to create a situation in which you can be as much at ease as possible. He will give instructions, tell you when to begin, check to see that you are marking your answer sheet correctly, and so on. He is not there to guard you, although he will see that your competitors do not take unfair advantage. He wants to help you do your best.

2) Listen to all instructions

Don't jump the gun! Wait until you understand all directions. In most civil service tests you get more time than you need to answer the questions. So don't be in a hurry. Read each word of instructions until you clearly understand the meaning. Study the examples, listen to all announcements and follow directions. Ask questions if you do not understand what to do.

3) Identify your papers

Civil service exams are usually identified by number only. You will be assigned a number; you must not put your name on your test papers. Be sure to copy your number correctly. Since more than one exam may be given, copy your exact examination title.

4) Plan your time

Unless you are told that a test is a "speed" or "rate of work" test, speed itself is usually not important. Time enough to answer all the questions will be provided, but this does not mean that you have all day. An overall time limit has been set. Divide the total time (in minutes) by the number of questions to determine the approximate time you have for each question.

5) Do not linger over difficult questions

If you come across a difficult question, mark it with a paper clip (useful to have along) and come back to it when you have been through the booklet. One caution if you do this – be sure to skip a number on your answer sheet as well. Check often to be sure that you have not lost your place and that you are marking in the row numbered the same as the question you are answering.

6) Read the questions

Be sure you know what the question asks! Many capable people are unsuccessful because they failed to read the questions correctly.

7) Answer all questions

Unless you have been instructed that a penalty will be deducted for incorrect answers, it is better to guess than to omit a question.

8) Speed tests

It is often better NOT to guess on speed tests. It has been found that on timed tests people are tempted to spend the last few seconds before time is called in marking answers at random – without even reading them – in the hope of picking up a few extra points. To discourage this practice, the instructions may warn you that your score will be "corrected" for guessing. That is, a penalty will be applied. The incorrect answers will be deducted from the correct ones, or some other penalty formula will be used.

9) Review your answers

If you finish before time is called, go back to the questions you guessed or omitted to give them further thought. Review other answers if you have time.

10) Return your test materials

If you are ready to leave before others have finished or time is called, take ALL your materials to the monitor and leave quietly. Never take any test material with you. The monitor can discover whose papers are not complete, and taking a test booklet may be grounds for disqualification.

VIII. EXAMINATION TECHNIQUES

1) Read the general instructions carefully. These are usually printed on the first page of the exam booklet. As a rule, these instructions refer to the timing of the examination; the fact that you should not start work until the signal and must stop work at a signal, etc. If there are any special instructions, such as a choice of questions to be answered, make sure that you note this instruction carefully.

2) When you are ready to start work on the examination, that is as soon as the signal has been given, read the instructions to each question booklet, underline any key words or phrases, such as least, best, outline, describe and the like. In this way you will tend to answer as requested rather than discover on reviewing your paper that you listed without describing, that you selected the worst choice rather than the best choice, etc.

3) If the examination is of the objective or multiple-choice type – that is, each question will also give a series of possible answers: A, B, C or D, and you are called upon to select the best answer and write the letter next to that answer on your answer paper – it is advisable to start answering each question in turn. There may be anywhere from 50 to 100 such questions in the three or four hours allotted and you can see how much time would be taken if you read through all the questions before beginning to answer any. Furthermore, if you

come across a question or group of questions which you know would be difficult to answer, it would undoubtedly affect your handling of all the other questions.

4) If the examination is of the essay type and contains but a few questions, it is a moot point as to whether you should read all the questions before starting to answer any one. Of course, if you are given a choice – say five out of seven and the like – then it is essential to read all the questions so you can eliminate the two that are most difficult. If, however, you are asked to answer all the questions, there may be danger in trying to answer the easiest one first because you may find that you will spend too much time on it. The best technique is to answer the first question, then proceed to the second, etc.

5) Time your answers. Before the exam begins, write down the time it started, then add the time allowed for the examination and write down the time it must be completed, then divide the time available somewhat as follows:
    - If 3-1/2 hours are allowed, that would be 210 minutes. If you have 80 objective-type questions, that would be an average of 2-1/2 minutes per question. Allow yourself no more than 2 minutes per question, or a total of 160 minutes, which will permit about 50 minutes to review.
    - If for the time allotment of 210 minutes there are 7 essay questions to answer, that would average about 30 minutes a question. Give yourself only 25 minutes per question so that you have about 35 minutes to review.

6) The most important instruction is to read each question and make sure you know what is wanted. The second most important instruction is to time yourself properly so that you answer every question. The third most important instruction is to answer every question. Guess if you have to but include something for each question. Remember that you will receive no credit for a blank and will probably receive some credit if you write something in answer to an essay question. If you guess a letter – say "B" for a multiple-choice question – you may have guessed right. If you leave a blank as an answer to a multiple-choice question, the examiners may respect your feelings but it will not add a point to your score. Some exams may penalize you for wrong answers, so in such cases only, you may not want to guess unless you have some basis for your answer.

7) Suggestions
    a. Objective-type questions
       1. Examine the question booklet for proper sequence of pages and questions
       2. Read all instructions carefully
       3. Skip any question which seems too difficult; return to it after all other questions have been answered
       4. Apportion your time properly; do not spend too much time on any single question or group of questions
       5. Note and underline key words – all, most, fewest, least, best, worst, same, opposite, etc.
       6. Pay particular attention to negatives
       7. Note unusual option, e.g., unduly long, short, complex, different or similar in content to the body of the question
       8. Observe the use of "hedging" words – probably, may, most likely, etc.

9. Make sure that your answer is put next to the same number as the question
10. Do not second-guess unless you have good reason to believe the second answer is definitely more correct
11. Cross out original answer if you decide another answer is more accurate; do not erase until you are ready to hand your paper in
12. Answer all questions; guess unless instructed otherwise
13. Leave time for review

b. Essay questions
1. Read each question carefully
2. Determine exactly what is wanted. Underline key words or phrases.
3. Decide on outline or paragraph answer
4. Include many different points and elements unless asked to develop any one or two points or elements
5. Show impartiality by giving pros and cons unless directed to select one side only
6. Make and write down any assumptions you find necessary to answer the questions
7. Watch your English, grammar, punctuation and choice of words
8. Time your answers; don't crowd material

8) Answering the essay question

Most essay questions can be answered by framing the specific response around several key words or ideas. Here are a few such key words or ideas:

M's: manpower, materials, methods, money, management
P's: purpose, program, policy, plan, procedure, practice, problems, pitfalls, personnel, public relations

a. Six basic steps in handling problems:
1. Preliminary plan and background development
2. Collect information, data and facts
3. Analyze and interpret information, data and facts
4. Analyze and develop solutions as well as make recommendations
5. Prepare report and sell recommendations
6. Install recommendations and follow up effectiveness

b. Pitfalls to avoid
1. Taking things for granted – A statement of the situation does not necessarily imply that each of the elements is necessarily true; for example, a complaint may be invalid and biased so that all that can be taken for granted is that a complaint has been registered
2. Considering only one side of a situation – Wherever possible, indicate several alternatives and then point out the reasons you selected the best one
3. Failing to indicate follow up – Whenever your answer indicates action on your part, make certain that you will take proper follow-up action to see how successful your recommendations, procedures or actions turn out to be
4. Taking too long in answering any single question – Remember to time your answers properly

EXAMINATION SECTION

EXAMINATION SECTION
TEST 1

DIRECTIONS: Each question or incomplete statement is followed by several suggested answers or completions. Select the one that BEST answers the question or completes the statement. *PRINT THE LETTER OF THE CORRECT ANSWER IN THE SPACE AT THE RIGHT.*

1. The Javadoc uses comments delimited by _____ to generate API doc. 1._____
   A. //   B. /*........*/   C. /**........*/   D. /*........**/

2. The _____ tag is used in comments to describe the parameter of the method. 2._____
   A. @param   B. @parameter   C. @describe   D. @since

3. When writing comments for a constructor, _____ tag cannot be used. 3._____
   A. @param   B. @return   C. @void   D. @deprecated

4. int a_ = 018;
   Why does the above statement generate error? 4._____
   A. Value is outside the range of int.
   B. Int cannot support values started with 0.
   C. Identifier is illegal.
   D. Number combination is wrong.

5. To deal with hexadecimal numbers, _____ data type is used. 5._____
   A. char   B. double   C. string   D. int

6. The range of _____ values are dependent on a virtual machine. 6._____
   A. short   B. long   C. Boolean   D. string

7. Floating point data types represent _____ numbers. 7._____
   A. real   B. primary   C. decimal   D. octal

8. String a = new String("hello");
   String b = "hello";
   Which one of the following statements is always evaluated to TRUE? 8._____
   A. a.equals(b)   B. a == b
   C. a.compareTo(b)   D. a.indexOf(b)

9. int i = 1, j = 2;
   int k = ++i+j++ + i++;
   What will be the result of k when evaluating the above expressions? 9._____
   A. 5   B. 10   C. 8   D. 6

10. ```
    int i, j = 1, k;
    i = 5;
    j = i++/2;
    k = i = j;
    ```
    What will be the result of k when evaluating the above expressions?
    A. 8   B. 2   C. 16   D. 4

11. 2 * -(+1) – (36/6 * 10) + (-20)/2
    What will be the result when the above expression is evaluated?
    A. -27   B. 72   C. -72   D. Syntax error

12. (2016%4) == 0? "leap year" : "year";
    What will be the output of the above expression?
    A. leap year   B. year   C. syntax error   D. runtime error

13. Which one of the following statements is FALSE?
    A. Logical '!' operator inverts a Boolean value.
    B. The unary bitwise operator inverts a bit pattern.
    C. In '&&' operator, both expressions are evaluated even if first if false.
    D. (/, *, %) operators have the same precedence.

14. long depth = 123456.89;
    What will happen when the above statement is compiled and executed?
    A. 123457 is assigned to depth.   B. 123456 is assigned to depth.
    C. Failed to compile.   D. Failed to run.

15. Consider the following block of code:
    ```
    int x = 1;
    int y = 1;

    if(!(true) && (x++<5) || (y++ < -15))

    y = x;
    if(!(10>12))
        x + = 10;

    y = x;
    if(!(x>1) && ((y*=2) > 3))
        x + = 200;

    System.out.println("x+" + x + "y=" + y);
    ```
    What will be the value of 'x' and 'y'?
    A. x = 211y = 11   B. x =11y = 11
    C. x = 1y = 1   D. Syntax error
    ```

16. 0x11+061+0x56
    What will be the result of k when evaluating the above expression?
    A. Failed to complete; cannot parse symbol x
    B. 10
    C. 8
    D. 152

17. char alpha = '@';
    alpha++;   //line1
    int beta = alpha;   //line2
    alpha = beta;   //line3
    beta = beta--;   //line4
    Which of the following statements causes compile time error?
    A. line1   B. line2   C. line3   D. line4

18. Which of the following is the CORRECT assignment?
    A. int a = 343.343;   B. long l = 98.9;
    C. Boolean b = 0;   D. float f = 45.0e3f;

19. if(!true || !false)
            System.out.println(true);
    else
            System.out.println(false);
    Which of the following blocks of code will be the output?
    A. Prints true   B. Prints false
    C. Program stuck in condition D. Syntax error

20. The FASTEST way to concatenate several strings is achieved by the _____ operator.
    A. minus (-)   B. dot (.)   C. plus (+)   D. quote (")

21. String str = "abc" + 123;
    System.out.println(str);
    Which of the following will be printed when the above line of code executes?
    A. Compile time error, cannot concatenate string with integer
    B. Compiled successfully and prints abc123
    C. Compiled successfully and prints abc
    D. Compiled successfully and prints 123

22. String str = "1" + "1";
    System.out.println(str);
    Which will be printed when the above line of code executes?
    A. Compile time error, cannot parse int as a String
    B. Compile time error, cannot add numeric as a String
    C. Compiled successfully and prints 11
    D. Compiled successfully and prints 1

23. Why is the performance of string concatenation dropped when concatenating thousands of string?
    A. The (+) operator takes time to merge
    B. As a string is immutable, a large number of objects are created in memory
    C. Because string includes numbers as well
    D. (+) operator fast is only with literals

    23.____

24. String s1 = new String();
    s1 = null;
    String s2 = "abc"
    System.out.println(s1+s2);   //line1
    System.out.println(s1.concat(s2));   //line2
    Considering the above block of code, what will be the output?
    A. Prints nullabc
    B. Prints abc
    C. Compiled time error at line 1
    D. Prints "nullabc" and throws NullPointerException at line 2

    24.____

25. Which one of the following statements is FALSE about String concatenation function?
    A. Only two strings can join at a time.
    B. Method concat throws NullPointerException when invoked on null object
    C. Method concat only takes a string object as argument.
    D. Method concat can take any object as argument.

    25.____

26. float f = 10.3E4f;
    Which of the following is the CORRECT way to convert the primitive float value into a String object? String s =
    A. new String(f);   B. (String)f;   C. f + " ";   D. f.toString();

    26.____

27. Which method of String class converts each letter of a string into UNICODE to compare two strings?
    A. compareTo   B. indexOf   C. equals   D. regionMatches

    27.____

28. When two objects share the same memory space, they are called
    A. equal   B. identical   C. duplicate   D. sibling

    28.____

29. When two objects have the same state, they are called
    A. equal   B. identical   C. duplicate   D. sibling

    29.____

30. Integer i = new Integer(1);
    Integer j = new Integer(2);
    Considering the above initializations, which of the following expressions compares contents and evaluates to a boolean value.
    A. i == j   B. i.compare(j)   C. i.equals(j)   D. i.compareTo(j)

    30.____

31. ArrayIndexOutOfBoundsException is directly descendent of the _____ class.
    A. Exception   B. IndexOutOfBoundsException
    C. StringOutOfBounds Exception D. RuntimeException

    31.____

32. String NULL = null;   //Line1
    String str = NULL;   //Line2
    Str.charAt(1);   //Line3
    Considering the above block of code, what will be the output?
    A. StringIndexOutOfBoundsException has thrown at line 3
    B. IllegalArgumentException has thrown at line 2
    C. Successfully compiles and prints 'u'
    D. NullPointerException has thrown at line 3

33. If the application is dealt with unevaluated input than _____, exception should be used to avoid errors.
    A. IllegalArgumentException   B. BadInputException
    C. MissingParameterException   D. MalformedException

34. Attempting to divide a float value from zero(0) results in a(n)
    A. ArthmeticException   B. 0
    C. infinity   D. 1

35. Which one of the following methods is used to print detail exception trace?
    A. printStackTrace   B. getMessage
    C. getDetail   D. printStack

36. System.out.println("\".length());
    When the above statement is executed, it throws compile time error because
    A. a length() method cannot be invoked on a string literal
    B. method length is undefined for type string
    C. the compiler takes (\) as an escape sequence and needs one more (') to close string properly
    D. compiler takes (\") as an escape sequence and needs one more (") to close string properly

37. Which of the following initializations throws compile time error?
    A. char[] arr = new char[] {'a','b','c','d'};
    B. int[] ar = new int[5];
    C. float[] a = {'a','b','c','d'};
    D. double [4]b = {'a','b','c','d'};

38. int[][] array = {{0},{0,0},{0,0,0},{o,o}};   //line1
    System.out.println(array.length + " " + array[array.length-3].length);   //line2
    Considering the above block of code, what will be the expected output?
    A. An IllegalArgumentException is thrown at line 2
    B. Prints 4 2
    C. Prints 4 3
    D. An ArrayIndexOutOfBoundsException is thrown at line 2

39. int[][] vals = {
    {1,2};
    {1,2,3};
    {4,5,6}
    };
    Considering the above block of code, what will be the expected result when executing vals[1][2]?
    A. 3   B. 6   C. 1   D. 4

    39.____

40. Considering the following table, declare and initialize its equivalent multi-dimensional array.

    40.____

1		2		3
1	2	3	4	5
1	2	3	5	
4				

A. int[][] testArray = {
    {1,0,2,0,3};
    {1,2,3,4,5};
    {1,2,3,5,0};
    {4}
    };

B. int[][] testArray = { {1,2,3,0,0};
    {1,2,3,4,5};
    {1,2,3,5,0};
    {4,0,0,0,0}
    };

C. int[][] testArray = { {1,2};
    {3,1,2,3,4,5};
    {1,2,3};
    };

B. int[][] testArray = {
    {1,2,3,4,5};
    {1,2,3,5};
    {4}
    };

Free Response Question

DIRECTIONS: The following is a free-response question, which requires you to demonstrate your ability to solve problems and analyze programs using Java. Show all work when answering the questions. (This question is modeled after the type of free-response questions found on the AP exam. Since there are different ways to answer the questions, there is no official answer provided.)

A set of classes is used to handle the different ticket types for a cinema. The class hierarchy is shown in the following diagram:

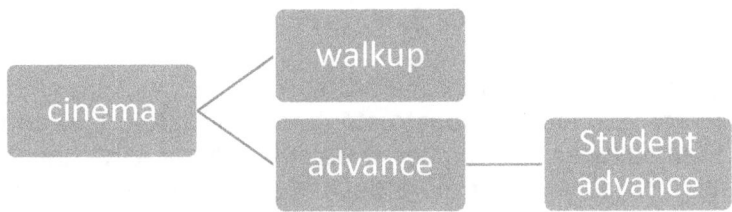

All tickets have a serial number and a price. The class ticket is specified as an abstract class as shown in the following declaration.

```
{
private int serialNumber; // unique ticket id number
public Ticket()
{
serialNumber = getNextSerialNumber();
}
// returns the price for this ticket
public abstract double getPrice();
// returns a string with information about the ticket
public String toString()
{
return "Number:" + serialNumber + "\nPrice: " + get Price();
}
// returns a new unique serial number
private static int getNextSerialNumber()
{/* implementation not shown*/}
}
```

Each ticket has a unique serial number. For all ticket classes, the toString method returns a string containing the information for that ticket. Three additional classes are used to represent the different types of tickets and are described in the table below.

Class	Description	Sample toString Output
Walkup	These tickets are purchased on the day of the event and cost 50 dollars.	Number: 712 Price: 50
Advance	Tickets purchased ten or more days in advance cost 30 dollars. Tickets purchased fewer than ten days in advance cost 40 dollars.	Number: 357 Price: 40
Student Advance	These tickets are a type of Advance ticket that costs half of what that Advance ticket would normally cost.	Number: 134 Price: 15 (Student ID required)

Using the class hierarchy and specifications given above, you will write complete class declarations for the Advance and StudentAdvance classes.

a. Write the complete class declaration for the class Advance. Include all necessary instance variables and implementations of its constructor and method(s). The constructor should take a parameter that indicates the number of days in advance that this ticket is being purchased. Tickets purchased ten or more days in advance cost $30; tickets purchased nine or fewer days in advance cost $40.

b. Write the complete class declaration for the class StudentAdvance. Include all necessary instance variables and implementations of its constructor and method(s). The constructor should take a parameter that indicates the number of days in advance that this ticket is being purchased. The toString method should include a notation that a student ID is required for this ticket. A StudentAdvance ticket costs half of what that Advance ticket would normally cost. If the pricing scheme for Advance tickets changes, the price should continue to be computed correctly with no code modifications to the StudentAdvance class.

KEY (CORRECT ANSWERS)

1.	C	11.	C	21.	B	31.	B
2.	A	12.	A	22.	C	32.	D
3.	B	13.	C	23.	B	33.	A
4.	A	14.	C	24.	D	34.	C
5.	D	15.	B	25.	D	35.	A
6.	C	16.	D	26.	C	36.	D
7.	A	17.	C	27.	A	37.	D
8.	A	18.	D	28.	B	38.	B
9.	D	19.	A	29.	A	39.	A
10.	B	20.	C	30.	C	40.	D

TEST 2

DIRECTIONS: Each question or incomplete statement is followed by several suggested answers or completions. Select the one that BEST answers the question or completes the statement. *PRINT THE LETTER OF THE CORRECT ANSWER IN THE SPACE AT THE RIGHT.*

1. ```
   int [][] vals = {  {2,2},
                      {1,2,3},
                      {4,5,6}
   };
   ```
   Considering the above multidimensional array, which of the following statements replaces the first row with new items?
   A. vals[2]]0] = 2;
   B. vals[2] = {4,5};
   C. int[] row = {(int)7.0,(int)8,0};   vals[2] = row
   D. vals[2] = new {4,5}[];

   1.____

2. Which of the following blocks of code populate array from square of the first 5 even numbers?
   A. ```
      int[] abc = new int[5];
      int counter = 0
      for(int a = 1; a ≤ 10; a++){
          abc[counter] = (a%2 == 0)? a*a : continue;
          counter++;
      }
      ```
   B. ```
      int[] abc = new int[5];
      for(int a = 1, counter = 0; a ≤ 10; a++){
          if(a%2 == 0){
              abc[counter] = a*a;
              counter++;
          }
      }
      ```
   C. ```
      int[] abc = new int[10];
      for(int a = 1, counter = 1; a ≤ 10; a++){
          if(a/2 == 0){
              abc[counter] = a*a;
              counter++;
          }
      }
      ```
   D. ```
      int[] abc = new int[5];
      int counter = 0;
      for(int a = 1, a ≤ 10; a++){
          if(a%2 == 0){
              abc[counter] = a*a;
          }
          counter++;
      }
      ```

   2.____
      ```

3.  ```
    int a = 5;
    int val = 1;
    for(int i = (a-1); i ≥ 0;){
       val = val*a;
       --i;
    }
    ```
    Considering the above block of code, what will be the value of val?
    A. 625 B. 1900 C. 3125 D. 4230

4.  ```
    public class Control{
       public static void main (String[] args){
          StringBuffer a = new StringBuffer("abc");
          changeIt(a);
          System.out.println(a.reverse());
       }
       public static void changeIt(StringBuffer s){
          s.append("-xyz");
          return;
       }
    }
    ```
    Considering the above class, what is the output of the above program?
    A. The program is successfully compiled and prints cba.
    B. The program is successfully compiled and prints abc – xyz.
    C. The program is successfully compiled and prints zyx – cba.
    D. The program is failed, as a method with return type does not have a return statement.

5. Considering the above program, which of the following is the INCORRECT statement?
    A. When changeIt method calls with argument 'a', it passes the value of 'a' as parameter.
    B. The empty return statement can be used in method having returned type void.
    C. When changeIt method calls with argument 'a', it passes memory the location of 'a' as parameter.
    D. Passing an argument, and modifying the same parameter results in modification of actual variable content

6. The _____ variable has the LEAST scope.
    A. local B. static C. instance D. transient

7. The _____ variable has the wider scope.
    A. local B. static C. instance D. transient

8. Encapsulation is achieved by making class data _____ and access them through methods.
    A. private B. public C. protected D. default

9. Considering a case when data of class are read only and cannot be set from outside the class, the CORRECT code fragment to achieve this is
    A. readonly String data;
    B. private String data;
       public static String getData(){
           return data;
       }
    C. private String data;
       public String getData (String data){
           return data;
       }
    D. private String data;
       public String getData(){
           return data;
       }
       private void setData(String data) {
           this,data = data;
       }

10. The data of the class are its private property. There should be a way to set data, but the postcondition is data must be validated against not more than 255 characters and greater than 3 characters. The CORRECT code fragment is
    A. private String data;
       public void setData(String data){
           if(data.length()>3 && data.length() ,= 255)
               this.data = data;
       }
    B. private String data;
       public void setData(String data){
           if(data.length() ≥ 3 II data.length() ,+ 255)
               this.data = data;
       }
    C. private String data;
       public void setData(String data){
           this.data = (data.length() ≥ 3 && data.length() ≤ 255) ? data : null;
       }
    D. private String data;
       public void setData(String data){
           this.data = (data.length() >3 && data.length() ? data : return;
       }

11. The class must only provide a way to initialize its object from a method. Which is the CORRECT statement to achieve this?
    A. The constructor is also a method to call it to create an object.
    B. Skip constructor and provide a static method to create an object.
    C. Make the constructor protected and provide a static method to create an object.
    D. Make the constructor private and provide a static method to create an object.

12. The class should have a class level string constant that has no accessibility restrictions. The CORRECT initialization using best practices is
    A. private static constant String CONSTANT = "constant";
    B. private static readonly String CONSTANT = "constant";
    C. public static final String CONSTANT = "constant";
    D. private static final String CONSTANT = "constant";

    12._____

13. The final instance variable cannot be initialized in the
    A. instance method   B. constructor
    C. instance block   D. at time of declaration

    13._____

14. Memory is allocated for _____ variables during class loading.
    A. instance   B. static   C. transient   D. volatile

    14._____

15. The objects cannot share their _____ variables with each other.
    A. volatile   B. transient   C. instance   D. final

    15._____

16. ```
    public class Animals {
        public static String type;
        public String name;

        public void print(){
            System.out.println(name+"is a" +type);
        }
        public static void main(String[] args){
            Animals dog = new Anikmals();
            dog.type = "Pet";
            dog.name = "Husky Dog";
            Animals cat = new Animals();
            cat.name = "Russian Cat";
            dog.print();
            cat.print()'
        }
    }
    ```
    What will be the output of the above class?
    A. Husky Dog is a Pet   B. Husky Dog is a Pet
       Russian Cat is a Pet   Russian Cat is a
    C. Russian Cat is a null   D. Husky Dog is a Pet
       Husky Dog is a Pet   Husky Dog is a Pet

    16._____

17. Considering the class in Question 16 above, if the statement (cat.type = "member";) is added before calling the print method, then what is the expected output?
    A. Husky Dog is a pet   B. Husky Dog is a pet
       Russian Cat is a member   Russian Cat is a pet
    C. Husky Dog is a member   D. Husky Dog is a member
       Russian Cat is a pet   Russian cat is a member

    17._____
    ```

18. John runs a tea café. He offers different types of tea like black milk tea, jasmine green tea, and chocolate milk tea. Each tea has some different ingredients. The ingredients of black milk tea are tea leaves, sugar, water, and milk. Jasmine tea is made up of jasmine leaves, sugar, and water. Chocolate milk tea has cocoa, milk, sugar, and ordinary tea leaves.
Which of the following writes an overloaded method of preparing tea?
Public void prepareTea(String sugar, int
   A. waterAndMilk, String teaLeaves){}
      water, String jasmineLeaves){}
      milk, String teaLeaves, String cocoa){}
   B. water, int milk, String teaLeaves){}
      water, String jasmineLeaves){}
      milk, String teaLeaves, String cocoa){}
   C. water, int milk, Striing teaLeaves){}
      water, int milk, String jasmineLeaves){}
      water int milk, String teaLeaves){}
   D. water, int milk, String teaLeaves, String flavor){}
      water, String jasmineLeaves, String honey){}
      milk, String teaLeaves, String cocoa){}

19. ```
    public class Tea {
        public static void prepareTea(String sugar, int water, int milk, String teaLeaves){
            if(milk == o)
                prepareTea(sugar, water, teaLeaves);
            else
                System.out.println("wow milk tea is ready");
        }
        public static void prepareTea(String sugar, int water, String teaLeaves){
            System.out.println("oh black tea");
        }
        public static void main(String args[]{
            prepareTea("2 spoon", 1, 0, "1 tablespoon tea leaves");
        }
    }
    ```
    What will be the output of the above program?
       A. prints 'oh black tea'
       B. prints 'wow milk tea is ready'
       C. failed to compile, but throws exception on runtime
       D. successfully compiled, but throws exception on runtime

20. Which one of the following methods in String class is overloaded?
       A. Length   B. Matches   C. Substring   D. Intern

21. Which one of the methods in Math class is NOT overloaded?
       A. Max   B. Min   C. Abs   D. Pow

22. Method overloading is NOT affected by _____ type.
       A. return   B. parameter   C. datatype   D. access
    ```

23. Which of the following components comprises a method signature? 23._____
    A. Return type, method name, and parameter types
    B. Access modifier, method name, and parameter types
    C. Method name and parameter types
    D. Method name, parameter types, and exception list

24. Which of the following elements are mandatory in method declaration? 24._____
    A. Method's return type, method name, parentheses() and a body between braces{}
    B. Method's return type, method name, and parentheses();
    C. Method name, parentheses() and a body between braces{}
    D. Access modifier, method's return type, method name, parentheses()

25. Which of the following method declaration elements are NOT considered in method overloading? 25._____
    A. Method's return type, exception list, and a body
    B. Method's return type, exception list, and parenthesis
    C. Method's name and parentheses
    D. Access modifier and method's name

26. Which of the following method declarations has all components (mandatory and optional)? 26._____
    A. Public void pickMe() {}
    B. Void pickMe(int a) {}
    C. Void pickMe(int a) throws Exception {}
    D. Private int pickMe() throws IOError {return 0;}

27. A list of variables in the method declaration is called 27._____
    A. arguments   B. parameters   C. lists   D. records

28. When the method is called the _____ are the actual vales pass into the method. 28._____
    A. parameters   B. references   C. arguments   D. pointers

29. Java passes the parameter as pass by 29._____
    A. value   B. reference   C. pointer   D. type

30. What types of methods cannot be overridden? 30._____
    A. Instance and final
    B. Final, private, and static
    C. Final, protected, and private
    D. Static and protected

31.
```
class SuperClass{
    public static void getDescription(){
        System.out.println("In SuperClass – getDescription");
    }
}
class SubClass extends MainClass{
    private static void getDescription(){
        System.out.println("In SubClass – getDescription");
    }
}
public class MainClass{
    public static void main(String args[]{
        SubClass.getDescriptionA();
        SuperClass.getDescription();
    }
}
```
Which of the following is the CORRECT statement?
   A. SuperClass method getDescription is overridden by SubClass method.
   B. When SubClass method getDescription invokes, it first calls its parent class getDescription method.
   C. The program is successfully compiled and prints:
      In SubClass – getDescription
      In SuperClass – get Description
   D. The program has failed to compile. SubClass cannot be called get Description method.

31.____

32.
```
class SuperClass{
    public float calc(inti , iknt j){
        return (i+j);                //Line1
    }
}
class SubClass extends SuperClass{
    public float calc(int i, int j){
        return (i*j);                //Line2
    }
}

public classMainClass{
    public static void main(String args[]{
        SuperClass superClass = new SuperClass();
        float val1 = superclass.calc(1,2);
        SubClass subclass = new SubClass();
        float val2 = subclass.calc(3,4);

        System.out.println(val1+"-"+val2);
    }
}
```

32.____

Which of the following is the CORRECT statement?
A. A program compiled successfully and prints 3.0 - 12.0.
B. A program compiled successfully and prints 1.0 – 4.0.
C. A program compiled successfully and prints 3 – 12.
D. Failed to convert int to float at Line1 and Line2.

33.
```
class SuperClass{
    public int calc(int i, int j){
        return (i+j);
    }
}
class SubClass extends SuperClass{
    public float calc(int i, int j){
        return (i*j);
    }
    public int calc(int i, int j){
        return(i*j);
    }
}
```
Which of the following is the CORRECT statement?
A. Method calc is an overloaded method in SubClass.
B. SubClass has failed to compile, as it has duplicate name methods.
C. Method calc with return type int in SubClass overrides SuperClass method.
D. SubClass cannot inherit with SuperClass.

33._____

34.
```
class SuperClass{
    public int calc(int i, int j){
        return(i+j);
    }
}
class SubClass extends SuperClass{
    public int calc(int i, int j){
        j = super.calc (i, j);
        return (i*j);
    }
}
public class MainClass{
    public static void main(String args[]){
        SubClass subclass = new SubClass();
        float val2 = subClass.calc(6,2);
        System.out.println(val2);
    }
}
```
What will be the output of the above code?
A. 48.0   B. 48   C. 12   D. 12.0

34._____

35.
```
class SuperClass{
    public void getMessage(){
        System.out.print("Hey 1 message");
    }
}
class SubClass extends SuperClass{
    protected void get Message(){
        System.out.print("Hey 2 message");
    }
}
public class MainClass{
    public static void main(String args[]){
        SubClass subClass = new SubClass();
        subClass.getMessage();
    }
}
```
Which of the following is the CORRECT statement?
A. A program compiled successfully and prints "Hey 2 message".
B. The method getMessage() from the type SuperClass is never used locally.
C. The method getMessage() from the type SubClass is not visible.
D. Cannot reduce the visibility of the inherited method getMessage() from SuperClass.

36.
```
class SuperClass{
    protected void printMe(){
        System.out.print("In SuperClass printMe()");
    }
}
class SubClass extends SuperClass{
    public void printMe(int a){
        System.out.print("In SubClass printMe()");
    }
}
public class MainClass{
    public static vid main(String args[]){
        SubClass subClass = new SubClass();
        subClass.printMe();
        subClass.printMe(2);
    }
}
```
What will be the output of the above code?
A. Cannot reduce the visibility of the inherited method printMe(int) from SuperClass.
B. Cannot override the method printMe(int).
C. Prints "In SuperClass printMe() in SubClass printMe()".
D. Prints "In SuperClass printMe() in SubClass printMe()2".

37. ```
    class SuperClass{
        public static void printMe(){
            System.out.print("In SuperClass printMe()");
        }
    }
    class SubClass extends SuperClass{
        private void printMe(){
            System.out.print("In SubClass printMe()");
        }
    }
    public class MainClass{
        public static void main(String args[]){
            SuperClass.printMe();
        }
    }
    ```
    What will be the output of the above code?
    A. Prints "In SuperClass printMe()".
    B. Cannot reduce the visibility of the inherited method printMe() from Superclass.
    C. Instance method printMe() cannot override the static method printMe() from SuperClass.
    D. Method printMe() from the type SubClass is not visible.

38. ```
    class SuperClass{
        public void checkException() throws java.io.FileNotFoundException{}
    }
    class SubClass extends SuperClass{
        public void checkException() throws java.net.URLClassLoader{}
    }
    ```
    Which of the following is the CORRECT statement?
    A. No exception of type URLClassLoader can be thrown.
    B. An exception URLClassLoader Exception is not compatible with throws clause in SuperClass.checkException().
    C. Classes compiled successfully.
    D. Exception is not considered in method overloading.

39. ```
    class TestClass{
        public static void printMe(){
            System.out.print("static overloaded");
        }
        public void printMe(String s){
            System.out.print("instance"+s);
        }
    }
    ```
    ```

```
public class MainClass{
    public static void main(String args[]){
        TestClass subClass = new TestClass();
        subClass.printMe("overloaded");
        subclass.printMe();
    }
}
```
What will be the output of the above code?
- A. Prints "instance overloaded static overloaded".
- B. Prints "overloaded static overloaded".
- C. Static method cannot overload instance method.
- D. Duplicate method printMe() in TestClass.

40. **precondition**: class name is Test
    class as default and two int arguments constructors
    Which of the following is the CORRECT constructor creation?
    - A. Class(){}Class(int i){}
    - B. Test(){}Test(int i, int i){}
    - C. Test(){}Test)int i, int j){}
    - D. Only one constructor is allowed

40.____

12 (#2)

Free Response Question

DIRECTIONS: The following is a free-response question, which requires you to demonstrate your ability to solve problems and analyze programs using Java. Show all work when answering the questions. (This question is modeled after the type of free-response questions found on the AP exam. Since there are different ways to answer the questions, there is no official answer provided.)

Periodically, a company processes the retirement of some of its employees. In this question, you will write functions to help the company determine whether an employee is eligible to retire and to process the retirement of all eligible employees. The Employee class is declared as follows:

```
class Employee
{
public:
int Age() const;
// returns the age (in years) of this employee
int YearsOnJob() const;
// returns the number of years this employee has worked
doubleSalary() const;
// returns the salary of this employee in dollars
int ID() const;
// returns unique employee ID number
// constructors, other member functions and data not shown };
```

The Company class is declared as follows.
```
class Company
{
public:
void ProcessRetirements();
// postcondition:  all retirement-eligible employees have been
// removed from empList; empList has been resized
// to reflect retirements;
// empList remains sorted by employee ID;
// salaryBudget has been updated to reflect remaining
// employees
// constructor and other public methods not shown
private:
bool EmployeeIsEligible(const Employee & emp) const;
// postcondition: returns true if emp is eligible to retire;
// otherwise, returns false
apvector<Employee> empList;
```

// empList.length() is the number of employees in this company
int retireAge; // minimum age to retire
int retireYears; // minimum years on job to retire
double retireSalary; // minimum salary to retire
double salaryBudget;
// total salary of all employees };

The data member empList is sorted in ascending order by employee ID. The total of all salaries is maintained in the data membersalaryBudget.

- a. An employee is eligible for retirement if s(he) meets at least two of the following requirements:
    1. The employee is at least retireAge years old.
    2. The employee has worked for at least retireYears.
    3. The employee's salary is at least retireSalary.

    Write the Company member function EmployeeIsEligible, which is described as follows. EmployeeIsEligible returns a Boolean value that indicates whether Employee emp is eligible for retirement, using the rules described above. Complete function EmployeeIsEligible below.
    bool Company::EmployeeIsEligible(const Employee & emp) const
    // postcondition: returns true if emp is eligible to retire;
    // otherwise, returns false

- b. Write the Company member function ProcessRetirements, which is described as follows. ProcessRetirements removes al retirement-eligible employees from the empList array, resizes (shrinks) empList as appropriate (maintaining its order by employee ID), and decreases salaryBudget to reflect the salary of the remaining employees. In writing ProcessRetirements, youmay call EmployeeIsEligible, specified in part (a). Assume that EmployeeIsEligible works as specified, regardless of what you wrote in part (a). Complete function ProcessRetirements below.
    void Company::ProcesRetirements()
    // postcondition: all retirement-eligible employees have been
    // removed from empList; empList has been resized
    // to reflect retirements;
    // empList remains sorted by employee ID;
    // salaryBudget has been updated to reflect remaining
    // employees

KEY (CORRECT ANSWERS)

1.	C	11.	D	21.	D	31.	D
2.	B	12.	C	22.	A	32.	A
3.	C	13.	A	23.	C	33.	B
4.	C	14.	B	24.	A	34.	A
5.	A	15.	C	25.	A	35.	D
6.	A	16.	A	26.	D	36.	C
7.	B	17.	D	27.	B	37.	C
8.	A	18.	B	28.	C	38.	A
9.	D	19.	A	29.	A	39.	A
10.	A	20.	C	30.	B	40.	C

TEST 3

DIRECTIONS: Each question or incomplete statement is followed by several suggested answers or completions. Select the one that BEST answers the question or completes the statement. *PRINT THE LETTER OF THE CORRECT ANSWER IN THE SPACE AT THE RIGHT.*

1.
```
classTest{
    Test(){
        System.out.println("Object is created");
    }
    Test(int i){
        System.out.println("Object is created with argument");
    }
    void Test(){
        this(3);
        System.out.println("in method");
    }
    public static void main(String args[]){
        Test test = new Test();
        test.Test();
    }
}
```
What will be the output of the above code?
   A. Failed to compile; a method has a constructor name.
   B. Runtime error; multiple constructor cannot be allowed
   C. Prints "Object is created in method".
   D. Failed to compile; constructor call must be the first statement in a constructor.

1.____

2.
```
class Test{
    Test(){
        System.out.print(0);
    }
    Test(int i){
        this();
        System.out.print(i);
    }
    Test(int i, int j){
        this(i);
        System.out.print(i+j);
    }
    public static void main(String args[]){
        new Test(1,2);
    }
}
```
What will be the output of the above code?
   A. 013   B. 023   C. 320   D. 310

2.____

3.
```
class Test{
    Test(){
        System.out.print(0);
    }
    Test(int i){
        this();
        System.out.print(i);
    }
    Test(int i, int j){
        this(j);
        System.out.print(i+j){
    }
    public static void main(String args[]){
        new Test(1,2);
    }
}
```
What will be the output of the above code?
A. 013   B. 023   C. 320   D. 310

3.____

4.
```
classTest{
    Test(int i){
        System.out.print(i);
    }
    Test(inti k, int j){
        this(j);
        System.out.print(i+j);
    }
    public static void main(String args[]){
        new Test();
    }
}
```
What will be the output of the above code?
A. Prints 0.
B. Prints 00.
C. Failed to compile; constructor Test() is undefined.
D. Failed to execute; cannot find default constructor.

4.____

5.
```
class SuperClass{
    SuperClass(int i){
        System.out.print("SuperClass Constructor 2");
    }
}
class SubClass extends SuperClass{
    SubClass(){
        System.out.print("SubClass Constructor");
    }
```

5.____

```
        SubClass(int i){
            System.out.print("SubClass Constructor 2");
        }
    }
    public class MainClass{
        public static void main(String args[]){
            new SubClass();
        }
    }
```
What will be the output of the above code?
   A. Failed to compile; implicit super constructor SuperClass() is undefined.
   B. Prints "SubClass Constructor".
   C. Prints "SubClass Constructor SuperClass Constructor 2".
   D. Prints "SuperClass Constructor 2 SubClass Constructor".

6.
```
    class SuperClass{
        SuperClass(){
            System.out.print("SuperClass Constructor");
        }
        SuperClass(int i){
            this();
            System.out.print("SuperClass Constructor 2");
        }
    }
    class SubClass extends Superclass{
        SubClass(){
            super(1);
            System.out.print("SubClass Constructor");
        }
        SubClass(int i){
            this();
            System.out.print("SubClass Constructor 2");
        }
    }
    public class MainClass{
        public static void main(String args[]){
        }
    }
```
What will be the output of the above code?
   A. Prints "SuperClass Constructor SubClass Constructor".
   B. Prints "SuperClass Constructor 2 SubClass Constructor".
   C. Prints "SuperClass Constructor SuperClass Constructor 2 SubClass Constructor".
   D. Failed to compile; recursive constructor calling is not allowed.

6.____

7. To create a class, a _____ keyword is used.
   A. new   B. class   C. public   D. abstract

7.____

8. A _____ keyword returns the reference of an object.   8.____
   A. new   B. instance   C. object   D. reference

9. A _____ keyword is used to refer other non-static members of a class.   9.____
   A. static   B. super   C. this   D. instance

10. int[] a = new int[-4];   10.____
    What will happen when following line compile and execute?
    A. Integer array initializes with length 0.
    B. Integer array initializes with length 4.
    C. Failed to compile; an array cannot be installed.
    D. NegativeArraySizeException is thrown at runtime.

11. ```
    public class Test{
        public static void printMe(){
            System.out.println("Print Me");
        }
        public static void main(String[] args){
            Test test = null;
            test.printMe();           //line1
        }
    }
    ```
    11.____

    What will be the output of the above program?
    A. Compiled to fail; null pointer is thrown at line 1.
    B. A NullPointerException is thrown at line 1.
    C. Prints "Print Me".
    D. Compiled to fail; object cannot refer to a static member.

12. ```
    public class Test {
        Test(){
            new Test();
            System.out.println("In Test");
        }
        public static void main(String[] args){
            new Test();
        }
    }
    ```
    12.____

    What will be the output of the above program?
    A. Prints "In Test".
    B. Prints "In Test in Test".
    C. Compiled to fail; cannot allow recursive calls.
    D. Exception StackOverflowError is thrown at runtime

13. ```
    class SuperClass{
        private int i;
        int j;
        protected int k;
        public int m;
    }
    class SubClass extends SuperClass{
        public void printMe(){
            System.out.println(i);          //line1
            System.out.println(j);          //line2
            System.out.println(k);          //line3
            System.out.println(m);          //line4
        }
    }
    public class MainClass{
        public static void main(String args[]){
            SubClass subClass = new SubClass();
            subClass.PrintMe();
        }
    }
    ```
    What will be the output of the above program?
    A. Failed to compile at line 1; field i is not visible.
    B. Failed to compile at line 3; field k is not visible.
    C. Prints '0000'.
    D. Prints '1111'.

14. Which one of the following inheritances is NOT supported in Java?
    A. Single   B. Multiple   C. Hybrid   D. Hierarchical

15. By default, every class in Java is a subclass of
    A. Lang   B. Enum   C. String   D. Object

16. Which one of the following statements is NOT valid for inheritance?
    A. Class does not inherit from multiple classes.
    B. Extends keyword is used to inherit class.
    C. Class can inherit itself.
    D. Parent class cannot call its child members.

17. Members with _____ modifier is visible within the package and in the subclass.
    A. default   B. public   C. protected   D. private

18. _____ members of the class are not inherited.
    A. Static   B. Instance   C. Local   D. Temporary
    ```

19. ```
    class SuperClass{
        static
        {
        System.out.print("Static Block – SuperClass,");
        }
        {
        System.out.print("Instance Block – SuperClass,");
        }
        SuperClass()
        {
        System.out.print("Constructor – SuperClass");
        }
    }
    class SubClass extends SuperClass{ }

    public class MainClass {
        public static void main(String args[]){
            new SubClass();
        }
    }
    ```
    What will be the output of the above program?
    A. Compiled and run, but prints nothing.
    B. Prints "Static Block – SuperClass, Instance Block – SuperClass, Constructor – SuperClass".
    C. Prints "Static Block – SuperClass, Constructor – Superclass".
    D. Prints "Instance Block – SuperClass, Constructor – SuperClass".

20. ```
    interface Testing{
        abstract static int pow(int i);
    }
    ```
    What will happen when the above interface is compiled?
    A. Interface compiled successfully.
    B. Failed to compile; static method cannot be abstract.
    C. Failed to compile; abstract method cannot be static.
    D. Failed to compile; only public and abstract method is allowed.

21. ```
    interface Testing{
        void printMe();
    }
    class SuperClass{
        public void printMe(){
        System.out.println("SuperClass Method");
        }
    }
    ```
    ```

```
class SubClass extends SuperClass implements Testing{ }
public class MainClass{
    public static void main(String args[]){
        SuperClass a = neew SubClass();
        a.printMe();
    }
}
```
What will be the output of the above program?
- A. Failed to compile; SubClass must implement the inherited abstract method Testing.printgMe().
- B. Failed to compile; method in printMe() from the type SuperClass is not visible.
- C. Prints "SuperClass Method".
- D. Prints nothing.

22.
```
interface Testing{
    public void printMe();
}
class SuperClass implements Testing{
    public void printMe(){
        this.printgMe("args");
        System.out.print("printMe 1");
    }
    void printMe(String s){
        System.out.print("printMe 2");
    }
}
class SubClass extends SuperClass implements Testing { }

public class MainClass{
    public static void main(String args[]){
        Testing a = new SuperClass();
        a.printMe();                        //line1
    }
}
```
What will be the output of the above program?
- A. Prints "printMe 2 printMe 1".
- B. Prints "printMe 1".
- C. Failed to compile; method printMe(String) is undefined for Testing.
- D. NoSuchMethodException is thrown at runtime on line 1.

22.____

23. When a superclass object refers to subclass object, it is called
- A. association
- B. polymorphism
- C. serialization
- D. composition

23.____

24. When the object type is identified at runtime, it is called _____ binding polymorphism.
- A. early
- B. static
- C. over
- D. late

24.____

25. A(n) _____ class cannot be instantiated.
    A. abstract   B. final   C. private   D. default

26. The purpose of a(n) _____ method is to give general idea so that subclasses implement them according to their requirements.
    A. native   B. final   C. abstract   D. local

27. ```
    abstract class SuperClass{
        public void printMe(){
            System.out.print("printMe 1");
        }
    }
    public class MainClass{
        public static void main(String args[]){
            SuperClass a = new SuperClass();
            a.printMe();
        }
    }
    ```
    What will be the output of the above program?
    A. Failed to compile; the abstract class does not have an abstract method.
    B. Failed to compile; cannot instantiate the type SuperClass.
    C. Failed to compile; non-abstract method is not permitted in abstract class.
    D. Prints "printMe 1".

28. ```
    abstract class TestingAbstract{
        abstract Boolean testingMethod(){
            System.out.println("Inside Method");
            return true;
        }
    }
    ```
    Which of the following statements is CORRECT?
    A. Abstract class must have a non-abstract method as well.
    B. Abstract method does not provide an implementation.
    C. Abstract method does not return a value.
    D. Abstract method must be protected.

29. In Java, the _____ is used to group similar interfaces, classes, and enums and also avoid naming conflict.
    A. merge   B. import   C. packaging   D. package

30. Package must be declared as a _____ statement in a file.
    A. first
    B. last
    C. first statement in a class
    D. blank

31. The relationship in which the object is a type of another object is called
    A. INSTANCE-OF
    B. ARE-A
    C. IS-A
    D. HAS-A

32. The relationship in which one object holds the reference of another object is called
    A. INSTANCE-OF
    B. ARE-A
    C. IS-A
    D. HAS-A

33. A null is a special _____ of the null type.
    A. keyword
    B. literal
    C. constant
    D. identifier

34. A list uses a _____ sort algorithm to maintain the order of their objects.
    A. merge
    B. bubble
    C. insertion
    D. binary

35.
```
public class MainClass{
    public static void main(String args[]){
        List<Number>arr = new ArrayList<>();         //line1
        arr.add(1);                                   //line2
        arr.add(1.0);                                 //line3
        arr.add(-2);                                  //line4

        System.out.println(arr.get(1) instance of Integer);   //line5
    }
}
```
What will happen when it compiles and executes?
    A. Failed to compile; empty diamond is not permitted at line1.
    B. Failed to compile; the method add(Number) in the type List<Number> is not applicable for the arguments int and float.
    C. Compiled successfully and prints true.
    D. Compiled successfully and prints false.

36. An employee is a special type of person. It has a name, ID designation and department in which he works. Furthermore, department is another entity that holds the information of departments across the organization. However, the department remains existing if any employee will leave office.
Which one of the following object initialization is CORRECT considering the above case?
    A. Department department = new Department("1", "Marketing");\
       Employee emp = new Employee("101", "John", department);
    B. Employee emp = new Employee("101", "John");
       //department object created in employee constructor
    C. Department department = new Department("1", "Marketing", new Employee());
    D. Person person = new Person(new Employee(), new Department());

37. What does the method size() of an ArrayList return?
    A. It returns how the capacity of an ArrayList.
    B. Method size() is undefined for ArrayList.
    C. It returns how many elements are currently stored in the ArrayList.
    D. It returns the total number of bytes taken by an object in memory.

38. How do you remove a collection of objects from an ArrayList? 38.____
    A. clearAll()   B. remove(int)
    C. remove(object)   D. removeAll(Collection)

39. Which one of the following packages is always imported in class? 39.____
    A. java.utils   B. java.lang
    C. java.net   D. java.io

40. How are the objects inserted in the List? 40.____
    A. Using index   B. Using key
    C. Using code   D. Using primitive

Free Response Question

DIRECTIONS: The following is a free-response question, which requires you to demonstrate your ability to solve problems and analyze programs using Java. Show all work when answering the questions. (This question is modeled after the type of free-response questions found on the AP exam. Since there are different ways to answer the questions, there is no official answer provided.)

Consider the following incomplete class that stores information about a customer, which includes a name and unique ID (a positive integer). To facilitate sorting, customers are ordered alphabetically by name. If two or more customers have the same name, they are further ordered by ID number. A particular customer is "greater than" another customer if that particular customer appears later in the ordering than the other customer.

```
public class Customer
{
// constructs a Customer with given name and ID number
public Customer(String name, int idNum)
{/*implementation not shown*/}
// returns the customer's name
public String getName()
{/*implementation not shown*/}
// returns the customer's id
public int getID()
{/*implementation not shown*/}
// returns 0 when this customer is equal to other;
// a positive integer when this customer is greater than other;
// a negative integer when this customer is less than other
public int compareCustomer(Customer other)
{/*to be implemented in part (a)*/}
// there may be fields, constructors, and methods that are not shown.}
```

a. Write the Customer method compareCustomer, which compares this customer to a given customer. Other Customers are ordered alphabetically by name, using the compareTo method of the String class. If the names of the two customers are the same, then the customers are ordered by ID number. Method compareCustomer should return a positive integer if this customer is greater than other customer, a negative integer if this customer is less than other customer, and 0 if they are the same.
For example, suppose we have the following Customer objects.

Customer c1 = new Customer ("Mac", 1001);
Customer c2 = new Customer ("Anderio", 1002);
Customer c3 = new Customer ("Mac", 1003);

The following table shows the result of several calls to compareCustomer.

Method Call Result
c1.compareCustomer(c1) =>0
c1.compareCustomer(c2) =>a positive integer
c1.compareCustomer(c3) =>a negative integer

Complete method compareCustomer below.
// returns 0 when this customer is equal to other;
// a positive integer when this customer is greater than other;
// a negative integer when this customer is less than other
public int compareCustomer (Customer other)

KEY (CORRECT ANSWERS)

1. D	11. C	21. C	31. C
2. B	12. D	22. A	32. D
3. B	13. A	23. B	33. B
4. C	14. B	24. D	34. C
5. A	15. D	25. A	35. D
6. C	16. C	26. C	36. A
7. B	17. C	27. B	37. C
8. A	18. A	28. B	38. D
9. C	19. B	29. D	39. B
10. D	20. D	30. A	40. A

TEST 4

DIRECTIONS: Each question or incomplete statement is followed by several suggested answers or completions. Select the one that BEST answers the question or completes the statement. *PRINT THE LETTER OF THE CORRECT ANSWER IN THE SPACE AT THE RIGHT.*

1. ```
   public class Test{
       public static void main(String args[]){
           int i, j;
           for(i=1, j=0; i<10;i++)J+=i;
           System.out,println(i);
       }
   }
   ```
   What is the input of the above program?
   A. 20   B. 9   C. 11   D. 10

   1.____

2. ```
   public class Test{
       public static void main(String[] args){
           int x=10, y=0;
           if(x && y){
               System.out.print("TRUE");
           }
           else{
               System.out.print("FALSE");
           }}}
   ```
   What is the output for the above program?
   A. True   B. False
   C. Compile time error   D. Runtime error

   2.____

3. ```
   public class Test{
       public static void main(String[] args){
           int x = 3, y = 4;
           switch(x+3){
               case 6: y = 0;
               case 7: y = 1;
               default: y+=1;
           }
       }
   }
   ```
   What is the value of Y after executing the switch statement?
   A. 0   B. 1   C. 2   D. 4

   3.____
   ```

4. ```
   char ch = 'a';
   switch(ch){
       case 'a':
       case 'A': System.out.print(ch); break;
       case 'b':
       case 'B': System.out.print(ch); break;
       case 'c':
       case 'C': System.out.print(ch); break;
       case 'd':
       case 'D': System.out.print(ch);
   }
   ```
   What is the result of the execution of the above switch statement?
   A. a   B. ab   C. abd   D. abcd

   4.____

5. ```
   public class Test{
       static public void main(String args[]){
           int i, j;
           for(j=1; j<4; j++){
               i%=j
                   System.out.println(j);
           }
       }
   }
   ```
   What of the following options is CORRECT for the above code?
   A. 123   B. 1231
   C. Infinite loop   D. Runtime error

   5.____

6. ```
   class Mazak{
       public static void main(String[] args){
           int i = 5;
           System.out.println(++i);
           System.out.println(i++);
       }
   }
   ```
   What is printed out?
   A. 5,6   B. 5,5   C. 6,6   D. 6,5

   6.____

7. ```
   public class Test{
       public static void main(String args[]){
           int i=0, j=2;
           do{
               i=++i;
               j--;
           }while(j>0);
           System.out.println(i);
       }
   }
   ```

   7.____

What is the output of the above code?
A. 0   B. 2   C. 1   D. Nothing

8. ```
public class Test{
2. public static void main(String{} args){
3.   int x = 0;
4.   //insert code here
5.   do{} while(x++<y);
6.   System.out.println(x);
7. }
}
```
Which of the following options should inset at line 4 to get 12 as output?
A. int y = x;   B. int y = 10;   C. int y = 11;   D. int y = 12;

9. ```
public class Mazak{
  public static void main(String[] args){
    Circle myCircle;
    myCircle.Area = 400;
    System.out.println("Circle area is" + myCircle.area());
  }
}
```
What will be the output of the above code?
A. Circle area is 400   B. Circle area is
C. Compilation error   D. Runtime error

10. ```
public class Test{
  public static void main(String[] args){
    int[] a = new int[0];
    System.out.print(a.length);
  }
}
```
What is the expected output?
A. 0                B. Compilation error
C. Runtime error    D. Blank screen

11. ```
public class Test{
  public static void main(String args[]){
    double[] myList = {1,5,5,5,5,1};
    double max = myList{0};
    int indexOfMax = 0;
    for(int i = 1; i < myList.length; i++){
      if(myList[i] > max){
        max = myList[i];
        indexOfMax = i;
      } }
    System.out.println(indexOfMax);  }}
```
Which of the following is the CORRECT output?
A. 0   B. 1   C. 2   D. 3

12. Which one of the following is the CORRECT method for array declaration?
    A. int [] myList = {
    B. int [] myList = (5,8,2);
    C. int myList [] [] = {4,9,7,0};
    D. int myList [] = {4,3,7};

13. ```
    public class Test{
        public static void main(String[] args){
            String s1 = args[1];
            String s2 = args[2];
            String s3 = args[3];
            String s4 = args[4];
            System.out.print("args[2] = " + s2);
        }
    }
    ```
    What will happen when the above is executed?
    A. args[2] = 2
    B. args[2] = 4
    C. args[2] = null
    D. An exception is thrown at runtime

14. ```
    public class Test{
        public static void main(String[] args){
            String test = "a1b2c3";
            String[]tokens = test.spllit("\\d");
            for(String s: tokens)
                System.out.print(s);
        }
    }
    ```
    What is the output of the above code?
    A. abc
    B. 123
    C. error
    D. Unhandled exception

15. ```
    public class Test{
        public static void main(String args[]){
            String s = "what";
            StringBuffer sb = new StringBuffer("what");
            System.out.print(sb.equals(s)+", "+s.equals(sb));
        }
    }
    ```
    What is the output of the above code?
    A. True false   B. True true   C. False false   D. False true

16. ```
    1. public class Test{
    2.     public static void main(String args[]){
    3.         Object myObj = new String[]{"one", "two", "three"};
    4.         {
    5.             for(String s: (String[] myObj)
    6.                 System.out.print(s + ".");
    7.         }
    8.     }
    9. }
    ```

What will be the output after execution of the above code?
- A. Compilation error
- B. Runtime error
- C. One, two, three
- D. Blank screen

17. Private constructor is special _____ constructor.   17._____
    - A. Singleton class
    - B. multiple classes
    - C. base class
    - D. instance

18.
```
public class Test{
    public static void main(String args[]){
        String str = null;
        if(str.length() == 0){
            System.out.print("1");
        }
        else if(str == null){
            System.out.print("2");
        }
        else{
            System.out.print("3");
        }
}}
```
    What is the result of the above code when executed?   18._____
    - A. Compilation error
    - B. An exception
    - C. 1 is printed
    - D. 2 is printed

19.
```
public class Profile{
    private Profile(int w) {//line 1
        System.out.print(w);
    }
    public static Profile() {//line 5
        System.out.print(10)
    }
    public static void main(String args[]){
        Profile obj = new Profile(50);
    }
}
```
    When the above code is executed, it gives a(n) _____ error.   19._____
    - A. compilation
    - B. runtime
    - C. execution
    - D. no

20.
```
public class Profile{
    private Profile(int w){
        System.out.print(w);
    }
    public static Profile(){
        System.out.print(10);
    }
    public static void main(String args[]){
        Profile obj = new Profile(50);     }}
```
    20._____

What is the output of the above code?
A. 0 B. 7
C. Compilation error D. 10

21.
```
public class Test{
    public static void main(String[] args){
        String value = "abc";
        changeValue(value);
        System.out.println(value);
    }
    public static void changeValue(String a){
        a = "xyz";
    }
}
```
The above is a piece of code using strings. When this is executed, what will be the output?
A. ab B. abc C. xz D. xyz

21.____

22.
```
public class Test{
    public static void printValue(int i, int j, int k){
        System.out.println("int");
    }
    public static void printValue(byte...b){
        System.out.println("long");
    }
    public static void main(String...args){
        byte b = 9;
        printValue(b,b,b);
    }
}
```
What is the result of the above program after execution?
A. long B. int C. b D. error

22.____

23.
```
class MyClass{
    MyClass(){
        System.out.print("one");
    }
    public void myMethod(){
        this();
        System.out.print("two");
    }
}
public class TestClass{
    public static void main(String args[]){
        MyClass obj = new MyClass();
        obj.myMethod();
    }
}
```

23.____

The output of the above code is
A. two one one
B. one one two
C. one Exception
D. compilation error

24. ```
public class Test{
    public static void main(String args[]){
        MyClass obj = new MyClass();
        obj. val = 1;
        obj. all(obj);
        System.out.println(obj. val);
    }
}
class MyClass{
    public int val;
    public void call(MyClass ref){
        ref.val++;
    }
}
```
What will be printed when the above code is executed?
A. 1
B. 4
C. 2
D. 0

25. The _____ class represents Character strings.
A. Java.lang.string
B. Java.text.string
C. Java.lang.class
D. Java.in

26. What is the CORRECT way of declaring constructor for public class MyClass{}?
A. MyClass()
B. MyClass(void){}
C. public MyClass(){}
D. public MyClass(void){}

27. ```
1. public class A{
2.     int add(int i, int j){
3.         return i+j;
4.     }
5. }
6. public class B extends A{
7.     public static void main(String args[]){
8.         short s = 9;
9.         System.out.println(add(s,6));
10.    }
11. }
```
In the above code snippet, why does the code fail to compile?
A. Error at line 2
B. Error at line 4
C. Error at line 8
D. Error at line 6

28. ```
    public class MotorA{
        public void methodOne(int i){
        }
        public void method(Two(int i){
        }
        public static void methodThree(int i){
        }
        public static void methodFour(int i){
        }
    }
    public class MotorB extends MotorA{
        public static void methodOne(int i){
        }
        public void methodTwo(int i){
        }
        public void methodThree(int i){
        }
        public static void methodFour(int i){
        }
    }
    ```
    Which type of error is detected in the above code?
    A. Runtime error
    B. Compile time error
    C. Exception
    D. Output is not shown

29. The finalize() method is called before
    A. an object; variable or method goes out of scope
    B. an object or variable goes out of scope
    C. a variable goes out of scope
    D. before garbage collection

30. The class at the top of exception class hierarchy is
    A. Arithmetic Exception
    B. Throwable
    C. Object
    D. Exception

31. ```
    public class Test{
        public static void main(String args[]){
            try{
                Striing arr[] = new String[10];
                arr = null;
                arr[0] = "one";
                System.out.print(arr[0]);
            }catch(Exception ex){
                System.out.print("exception");
            }catch(NullPointerException nex){
                System.out.print("null pointer exception");
            }
        }
    }
    ```

What error occurs when the above code is executed?
A. Null pointer exception
B. Compilation fails saying nullpointerexception has already been caught
C. Runtime error
D. compile time error

32.
```
Class A{
    public void doA(){
        B b = new B();
        b.dobB();
        System.out.print("doA");
    }
}
class B{
    public void dobB(){
        C c = new C();
        c.doC();
        System.out.print ("doB");
    }
}
class C{
    public void doC(){
        if(true)
            throw new NullPointerException();
        System.out.print("doC");
    }
}
public class Test{
    public static void main(String args[]){
        try{
            A a = new A();
            a.doA();
        }catch(Exception ex){
            System.out.print("error");
        }
    }
}
```
What is the output of the above code?
A. doCdoBdoA   B. doCdoB
C. Error   D. Compilation error

33.
```
try{
    File f = new File("a.txt");
}catch(Exception e){
}catch(IOException io){
}
```
What is TRUE for the above code?
A. Txt file is created   B. Execution error
C. Compile time error   D. Class name is invalid

34. ```
    public class Test{
        public void divide(int a, int b){
            try{
                int c = a/b;
            }catch(Exception e){
                System.out.print("Exception");
            }finally{
                System.out.println("Finally");
            }
        }
        public static void main(String args[]){
            Test t = new Test();
            t.divide(0,3);
        }
    }
    ```
    What is the possible outcome of the above code?
    A. Exception
    B. Exception Finally
    C. Compile with error
    D. Finally

    34.____

35. ```
    interface A{
        public void printValue();
    }
    1.  public class Test{
    2.      public static void main(String[] args){
    3.          A a1 = new A(){
    4.              public void printValue(){
    5.                  System.out.println("A");
    6.              }
    7.          };
    8.          a1.printValue();
    9.      }
    10. }
    ```
    What is the output of the above piece of code?
    A. A
    B. Null
    C. 0
    D. Blank screen

    35.____

36. ```
    public interface TestInf{
        int i = 10;
    }
    public class Test{
        public static void main(String...args){
            Testinf.i = 12;
            System.out.println(TestInf.i);
        }
    }
    ```
    What is the result of the above code after execution?
    A. 10
    B. 12
    C. Runtime error
    D. Compile time error

    36.____
    ```

37. ```
    public class Test implements Runnable{
        public void run(){
            System.out.print("go");
        }
        public static void main(String arg[]){
            Thread t = new Thread(new Test());
            t.run();
            t.run();
            t.start();
        }
    }
    ```
    What is the output of the above program?
    A. go   B. gogo   C. gogogo   D. error

38. ```
    public class Test implements Runnable{
        public static void main(String[] args) throws Interrupted Exception{
            Thread a =new Thread(new Test());
            a.start();
            System.out.print("start");
            a.join();
            System.out.print("effort");
        }
        public void run(){
            System.out.print("daily");
        }
    }
    ```
    What is printed when the above code is executed?
    A. starteffortdaily
    B. starteffort
    C. start
    D. startdailyeffort

39. ```
    class Base{
        private Base(){
            System.out.print("Base");
        }
    }
    public class test extends Base{
        public test(){
            System.out.print("Derived");
        }
        public static void main(String[] args){
            new test();
        }
    }
    ```
    What will happen when the above code is executed?
    A. Runtime error
    B. Exception
    C. Compile time error
    D. Normal run
    ```

40. ```
public class Test{
    static int a;
    public static void main(String[] args){
        System.out.println("one");
        call(1);
    }
    static void call(int a){
        this.a = 10;
        System.out.println("Two" +a);
    }
}
```
What is the result of the above code after execution?
A. Compile time error
B. one two 0
C. one two 1
D. Runtime error
```

13 (#4)

Free Response Question

DIRECTIONS: The following is a free-response question, which requires you to demonstrate your ability to solve problems and analyze programs using Java. Show all work when answering the questions. (This question is modeled after the type of free-response questions found on the AP exam. Since there are different ways to answer the questions, there is no official answer provided.)

The menu at a restaurant includes a variety of sandwiches, salads, and drinks. The menu also allows a customer to create a "deal," which consists of three menu items: a sandwich, a salad, and a drink. The price of the deal is the sum of the two highest-priced menu items in the deal, one item with the lowest price is free. Each menu item has a name and a price. The four types of menu items are represented by the four classes Sandwich, Salad, Drink, and Deal. All four classes implement the following MenuItem interface.

public interface MenuItem{
double getprice()
// returns name of the menu item
// returns price of the menu item
}

The following diagram shows the relationship between the MenuItem interface and the Sandwich, Salad, Drink, and Deal classes.

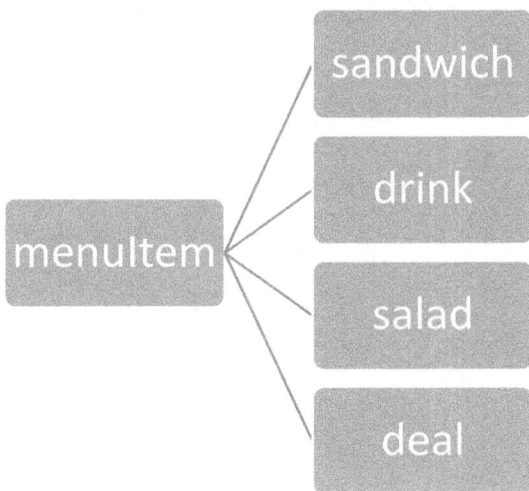

14 (#4)

For example, assume that the menu includes the following items. The objects listed under each heading are instances of the class indicated by the heading.

Sandwich
cheeseburger 2.75
club sandwich 7.72
Drink
Orange soda 1.25
Mint soda 3.50
Salad
spinach salad 1.25
coleslaw 1.25

The menu allows customers to create deal menu items, each of which includes a sandwich, a salad, and a drink. The name of the deal consists of the names of the sandwich, salad, and drink, in that order, each separated by "/" and followed by a space and then "deal". The price of the deal is the sum of the two highest-priced items in the deal; one item with the lowest price is free.

A deal consisting of a cheeseburger, spinach salad, and an orange soda would have the name "cheeseburger/spin salad/orange soda deal" and a price of $4.00 (the two highest prices are $2.75 and $1.25). Similarly, a deal consisting of a club sandwich, coleslaw, and a cappuccino would have the name "club sandwich/coleslaw/min soda deal" and a price of $6.25 (the two highest prices are $2.75 and $3.50).

Write the deal class that implements the MenuItem interface. Your implementation must include a constructor that takes three parameters representing a sandwich, salad, and drink.

KEY (CORRECT ANSWERS)

1.	D	11.	B	21.	B	31.	B
2.	C	12.	D	22.	B	32.	D
3.	C	13.	D	23.	D	33.	D
4.	A	14.	A	24.	C	34.	C
5.	C	15.	C	25.	A	35.	A
6.	C	16.	C	26.	C	36.	D
7.	B	17.	D	27.	D	37.	C
8.	C	18.	B	28.	B	38.	D
9.	C	19.	A	29.	D	39.	C
10.	A	20.	C	30.	B	40.	A

TEST 5

DIRECTIONS: Each question or incomplete statement is followed by several suggested answers or completions. Select the one that BEST answers the question or completes the statement. *PRINT THE LETTER OF THE CORRECT ANSWER IN THE SPACE AT THE RIGHT.*

1. String cloud = new String("America");
    System.out.println(cloud.length());
   What is the output of the above code?
   A. 6   B. 7   C. 8   D. America

   1.____

2. public class MyClass{
       public MyClass()
   {/*code*/}
   //more code...}
   To instantiate MyClass, what will you write?
   A. MyClass mc = new MyClass();   B. MyClass mc = MyClass();
   C. MyClass mc = MyClass;   D. MyClass mc = new MyClass;

   2.____

3. public class StringToUpperCaseEmp{
       public static void main(String[] args){
           String str = "java is programming language";
           String strUpper = str.toUpperCase();

           System.out.println("string is:" + strUpper);
       }}
   What is the CORRECT output of the given code?
   A. Java is programming language.
   B. String is :java is programming language
   C. String is :JAVA IS PROGRAMMING LANGUAGE
   D. Java Is Programming Language

   3.____

4. Which of the following is the CORRECT code to count array size?
   A. public class ArraySize{
          public static void main(String[] args){
              Integer[] arrayExample = Integer[] {1,2,3};
              System.out.println("Array Size is: "+arrayExample.Int); }}
   B. public class ArraySize{
          public static void main(String[] {1,2,3};
              Integer[] arrayExample = new Integer[] {1,2,3};
              System.out.println("Array Size is:"+arrayExample.length); }}
   C. public class ArraySize{
      public static void main(String[] args) {
      Integer[] arrayExample = new Integer[] {1,2,3};
      System.out.println("ArraySize is:"+arrayExample); }}
   D. public class ArraySize{
      public static void main(String[] args){
      Integer[] arrayExample = new Integer[] {1,2,3};
      System.out.println("Array Size is:"+length); }}

   4.____

5. public class SortArrayListExample{
   public static void main(String[] args){
   ArrayList<String>profession = new ArrayList<String>();
   profession.add("Teacher");
   profession.add("Army");
   profession.add("Peon");
   profession.add("Sweaper");
   Collections.sort(profession);
   for(String s:profession){
   System.out.println(s); }
   Collections.sort(list,C(); }}
   The expected output of the above code is
   A. Army, Peon, Seaper, Teacher B. ARMY, PEON, SEAPER, TEACHER
   C. 4   D. compilation error

6. public class Test{
       public static void main(String args[]){
           String s1 = new String("Home");
           String s2 = new String("Whome");
           System.out.println(s1 = s2); }}
   The output of the above code is
   A. Compilation error   B. An exception
   C. Home   D. Whome

7. class LogicalCompare{
       public static void main(String args[]){
           String str1 = new String("OKAY");
           String str2 = new String(str1);
           System.out.println(str1 == str2);
       }}
   The CORRECT output for the above code is
   A. True   B. False   C. 1   D. 0

8. Which one of the following is the CORRECT piece of code?
   A. public class Test{
          public static void main(String args[]){
              String s1 = "Bob";
              String s2 = "Alice";
              System.out.println(s1.charAt(0)>s2.charAt(0)); }}
   B. public class Test{
          public static void main(String args[]){
              String s1 = 'Bob';
              String s2 = 'Alice';
              System.out.println(s1.charAt>s2.charAt); }}
   C. public class test{
          public static void main(String args[]){
              String s1 = 'Bob';
              System.out.println(s1.charAt(0)>s2.charAt(0)); }}

D. public class Test{
      public static void main(Strinig args[]){
        String s1 = Bob;
        String s2 = Alice;
        System.out.println(s1.charAt(0)>s2.charAt(0)); }}

9. toString() method is defined in
   A. java.lang.object
   B. java.lang.util
   C. java.lang.String
   D. Both A and B

10. String str1 = "uvxyz";
    System.out.println(str1.substring(1,3));
    What is the CORRECT output for the above code?
    A. uvxyz   B. vx   C. xyz   D. yz

11. What is the CORRECT piece of code if you want to join two strings?
    A. public class Test{
         public static void main(String args[]){
           String str1 = "one";
           String str2 = "two";
           System.out.println(str1 + (str2)); }}
    B. public class Test{
         public static void main(String args[]){
           String str1 = one;
           String str2 = two;
           System.out.println(str1.concat(str2)); }}
    C. public class Test{
         public static void main(String args[]){
           String str1 = "one";
           String str2 = "two";
           System.out.println(str1.concatstr2); }}
    D. public class Test{
         public static void main(String args[]){
           String str1 = "one";
           String str2 = "two";
           System.out.println(str1.concat(str2)); }}

12. String str1 = "Karma".replace('k', 'a');
    What is the effect of the above string?
    A. All characters k are replaced by a
    B. Error message
    C. Only first occurrence of k is replaced by a
    D. All characters a are replaced by k

13. After executing int ++a = 100; System.out.println(++a);
    what message will appear?
    A. 102
    B. 100
    C. ++a is not a valid identifier
    D. ++a is not enclosed in double quotes

14. ```
    class Numbers{
        public static void main(String args[]){
            int a = 20, b = 10;
            if((a<b) && (b++<25)){
                System.out.println("This is any language logic");
            }
            System.out.println(b);
        }
    }
    ```
    What number will be displayed when the above piece of code is executed?
    A. Error   B. 10   C. 20   D. 27

15. Which one of the following code returns true value?
    A. ```
       if(1+1+1+1+1 = = 5){
           System.out.print("TRUE");
       }
       else{
           System.out.print("FLASE");
       }
       ```
    B. ```
       if(1+1+1+1+1!=5){
           System.out,print("TRUE");
       }
       else{
           System.out.print("FLASE");
       }
       ```
    C. ```
       if(1+1+1+1+1>5){
           System.out.print("TRUE");
       }
       else{
           System.out.print("FLASE");
       }
       ```
    D. ```
       if(1+1+1+1+1<5){
           System.out.print("TRUE");
       }
       else{
           System.outprint("FLASE");
       }
       ```

16. Which one of the following is the CORRECT expression for x is between 1 and 100 or the x is negative?
    A. ((x<100) && (x>1)) II (x<0)   B. (1>x>100) II (x<0)
    C. ((x<100) && (x>1)) && (x<0)   D. 1<x<1—II x<0

17. ```
    public class Test{
        Test() { } // line 1
        static void Test() { this(); } // line 2
        public static void main(String[] args) { // line 3
            Test(); // line 4
        }}
    ```

Which of the follow lines has the error?
A. At line 1
B. At line 1 and 2
C. Only at line 4
D. At line 3

18. Which of the following is the BEST possible option to generate random integers from 0 to 100?
    A. (int)(Math.random()+0.5)
    B. (int)Math.random()+0.2
    C. (int)Math random()+1
    D. (int)Math.random()

19. _____ modifier cannot be used for constructors.
    A. Public
    B. Static
    C. Private
    D. Protected

20. ```
    public class Test{
        public static void main(String args[]){
            System.out.println(Math.floor(Math.random()));
        }
    }
    ```
    What is the output of the above code?
    A. 0.5
    B. 1
    C. 0.0
    D. 10.0

21. _____ package contains system class that is defined in it.
    A. Java.lang
    B. Java.io
    C. Java.util
    D. Java.awt

22. Which of the following classes defined in java.io and used for file handling are abstract?
    A. InputStream,Reader
    B. PrintStream,Reader
    C. Reader, FileWriter
    D. FileImputStream

23. If a class extends the Thread class, it is compulsory to override the _____ method of Thread class in order to start that thread.
    A. go()
    B. init()
    C. run()
    D. start()

24. ```
    public class Test implements Runnable{
        public static void main(String[] args){
            Thread t = new Thread(this);
            t.start();
        }
        public void run(){
            System.out.println("test");
        }
    }
    ```
    What is the output for the above code?
    A. Compilation error because this cannot be referenced in a static method.
    B. Nothing will be printed after successful compilation.
    C. The program compiles and runs fine and displays test on the console.
    D. Test

25. For thread class only, _____ constructor is valid.
    A. Thread(Runnable threadOb, int priority)
    B. Thread(int priority)
    C. Thread(Runnable threadOb, String threadName)
    D. Thread(String threadName, int priority)

26. ```
    public class Test implements Runnable{
        public static void main(String[] args){
            Test t = new Test();
            t.start();
        }
        public void run() { }
    }
    ```
    What is the output of the above code?
    A. The program runs fine.
    B. The program compiles and doesn't show any output.
    C. The program does not compile.
    D. Blank screen

27. ```
    1. public class Test extends Thread{
    2.     public static void main(String arg[]){
    3.         Test t = new Test();
    4.         t.run();
    5.         t.start();
    6.     }
    7.     public void run(){
    8.         System.out.println("run-test");
    9.     }
    10. }
    ```
    What is the expected output for the above code fragment?
    A. Compilation error at line 9   B. Compilation error at line 3
    C. Run test run test   D. Run test

28. _____ methods are used for thread class.
    A. yield(), sleep(long msec), stop()   B. sleep(long msec)
    C. go(), stop()   D. stop(), yield()

29. _____ keyword makes sure when applied on a method that only single thread should execute the method at a time.
    A. Final   B. Static   C. Native   D. Synchronized

30. Which of the following statements are CORRECT?
    I. A class can extend more than one class.
    II. A class can extend only one class but many interfaces.
    III. An interface can extend many interfaces.
    IV. An interface can implement many interfaces.
    V. A class can extend one class and implement many interfaces.
    The CORRECT answer is:
    A. II and III   B. III and V   C. I and V   D. IV and V

31. In java multiple inheritance concept is implemented by
    A. implementing two or more interfaces
    B. implementing one interface
    C. extending two or more classes
    D. extending one class

32. ```
    class Parent{
        public void method(){
            System.out.println("Hi i am programmer");
        }
    }
    public class Child extends Parent{
        protected void method(){
            System.out.println("Hi i am engineer");
        }
        public static void main(String args[]){
            Child child = new Child();
            child.method();
        }
    }
    ```
    What happens when the above piece of code is executed?
    A. Runtime error   B. Compile time error
    C. Program runs successfully   D. Execution error

33. ```
    class A{
        A(String s){ }
        A(){ }
    }
    1.  class B extends A{
    2.      B(){ }
    3.      B(String s){
    4.          super(s);
    5.      }
    6.      void test(){
    7.          //insert code here
    8.      }
    9.  }
    ```
    Which code should be added in line 7 to run this program successfully?
    A. Aa = new B();   B. Aa = new B(5);
    C. Aa = new A(String s); D. Aa = new(string)

34. _____ declares an abstract method in an abstract Java class?
    A. public abstract method();   B. public abstract void method();
    C. public void abstract Method();   D. public void method()

35. Which of the following class definitions defines a legal abstract class?
    A. class A {abstract void unfinished(){ } }
    B. class A {abstract void unfinished();}
    C. abstract class A {abstract void unfinished();}
    D. public class abstract A {abstract void unfinished();}

36. ```
    interface Test{
        int p = 10; //line 1
        public int q = 20; //line 2
        public static = 30; //line 3
        public static final int s = 40; //line 4
    }
    ```
    Which of the following lines shows an error?
    A. Line 2   B. Line 3   C. Line 1   D. Line 4

37. ```
    public class Test{
        public static void main(String args[]){
            int i;
            for(i = 1; i<6; i++){
                if(i>3) continue;
            }
            System.out.println(i);
        }
    }
    ```
    What is the output of the above code?
    A. 5   B. 6   C. 2   D. 1

38. In Java _____ can only test for equality, whereas _____ can evaluate any type of the Boolean expression.
    A. switch, if
    B. if, switch
    C. if, break
    D. continue, if

39. ```
    public class Test{
        public static void main(String args[]){
            int i = 0, j = 5;
            for(;(i<3) && (j++<10); i++){
                System.out.print(" " +i+" "+j);
            }
            System.out.print(" "+i+" "+j);
        }
    }
    ```
    Which of the following is the expected output for the given code?
    A. 0 6 1 7 2 8 3 8
    B. 0 6 1 7 2 8 3 9
    C. 0 6 1 5 2 5 3 5
    D. Compilation error
    ```

40. ```
    class Test{
        public static void main(String args[])}
            int x = 7;
            if(x == 2);
            System.out.println("NumberSeven");
            System.out.println("NotSeven");
    }}
    ```
    What is the result of this program when executed?
    A. NumberSeven NotSeven
    B. NumberSeven
    C. NotSeven
    D. Error

40.____
    ```

Free Response Question

DIRECTIONS: The following is a free-response question, which requires you to demonstrate your ability to solve problems and analyze programs using Java. Show all work when answering the questions. (This question is modeled after the type of free-response questions found on the AP exam. Since there are different ways to answer the questions, there is no official answer provided.)

This question includes the design of an interface, writing a class that implements the interface. A number group represents a group of integers defined in some way. It could be empty, or it could contain one or more integers. Write an interface named NumberGroup that represents a group of integers. The interface should have a single contains method that determines if a given integer is in the group. For example, if group1 is of type NumberGroup, and it contains only two numbers -5 and -3, then group1.contains (-5) would return true, and group1.contains(2) would return false. Write the complete NumberGroup interface. It must have exactly one method.

KEY (CORRECT ANSWERS)

1.	B	11.	D	21.	A	31.	A
2.	A	12.	A	22.	A	32.	B
3.	C	13.	C	23.	C	33.	A
4.	B	14.	B	24.	A	34.	B
5.	D	15.	A	25.	C	35.	C
6.	D	16.	A	26.	C	36.	B
7.	B	17.	D	27.	A	37.	B
8.	A	18.	A	28.	A	38.	A
9.	A	19.	B	29.	D	39.	A
10.	B	20.	C	30.	B	40.	A

EXAMINATION SECTION
TEST 1

DIRECTIONS: Each question or incomplete statement is followed by several suggested answers or completions. Select the one that BEST answers the question or completes the statement. *PRINT THE LETTER OF THE CORRECT ANSWER IN THE SPACE AT THE RIGHT.*

1. Computer language is best described as a
   A. pattern   B. set of rules   C. sign   D. way to communicate
   1.____

2. The _____ is the instructions for a computer to complete a task.
   A. function   B. statement   C. program   D. delimiter
   2.____

3. The set of rules required to write a correct program is called
   A. instructions   B. semantics   C. syntax   D. language
   3.____

4. Assembly language uses _____ to write code.
   A. mnemonics
   B. binary 0s and 1s
   C. English
   D. symbols
   4.____

5. Which of the following data types is supported by a switch statement?
   A. Double   B. Float   C. Char   D. Boolean
   5.____

6. Which is an invalid operator in Java?
   A. !   B. >?   C. ==   D. !=
   6.____

7. ```
   public class Test{
       public static void main(String[]args){
       char a = 'a';
       int b = 97;
       String result = (a == b) ? "Equal" : "Not Equal";
       System.out.println(result);
       }
   }
   ```
   What is the output of the above code?
   A. Equal   B. Not Equal
   C. Compile-time error   D. Runtime error
   7.____

8. Which one of the following data types is returned by (≥) relational operator?
   A. int   B. boolean   C. char   D. float
   8.____

9. A class having two methods with the same name but different parameters is called
   A. Overloading   B. Overriding
   C. Hiding   D. Extending
   9.____
   ```

10. Method Overloading is resolved at
    A. Calling time
    B. Runtime
    C. JVM start
    D. Compile-time

11. Which one of the following statements is TRUE when passing an argument by value?
    A. The argument's copy is passed to a method parameter.
    B. Initial argument's reference is passed to a method parameter.
    C. The argument's copy is passed to a method parameter and changes made on parameter effects the original argument.
    D. Initial argument's reference is passed to a method parameter and changes made on parameter effects the original argument.

12. _____ overloading is not supported in Java.
    A. Method   B. Operator   C. Variable   D. Constructor

13. _____ operator is used to initialize an array.
    A. Creat   B. Malloc   C. New   D. Init

14. Which of the following array utilizations is INCORRECT?
    A. int array{} = int [10]
    B. int array [] = new int[10]
    C. int [] array = new int[10]
    D. int array [] array = new int[10]

15. ```
    public class Array Test{
        public static void main(String args[]){
            int sequence[] = new int[10];
            for (int a = 0; a < 10; ++a) {
                a++;
                sequence[a] = a;
                System.out.print(sequence[a] + "");
            }
        }
    }
    ```
    What will be the output of the above program?
    A. 0 1 2 3 4 5 6 7 8 9
    B. 1 2 3 4 5 6 7 8 9 10
    C. 0 2 4 6 8
    D. 1 3 5 7 9

16. An array is a(n) _____ in Java.
    A. object   B. primitive   C. value   D. constraint

17. The _____ defines multiple objects of the same type.
    A. new   B. interface   C. class   D. variable

18. The _____ is the real world entity having properties and actions.
    A. method   B. variable   C. aspect   D. object

19. The _____ is used to invoke an object.
    A. method   B. thread   C. constructor   D. destructor
    ```

20. How do you keep class from being instantiated?
    A. Add static final constructor
    B. Add non-argument constructor with protected modifier
    C. Mark constructor abstract
    D. Mark constructor private

21. Which of the following packages contains classes and interfaces for IO operations?
    A. javax.io   B. java.net   C. java.socket   D. java.io

22. Which of the following is NOT true for File object usage?
    A. To rename the file
    B. To interact with the content of file
    C. To get the properties of file
    D. To delete the file

23. The class used to write file content is called a
    A. Scanner   B. System   C. String   D. PrintWriter

24. The class used to read file content is called a
    A. String   B. System   C. Scanner   D. PrintWriter

25. When an array is passed as a method argument, the method receives the parameter as a(n)
    A. array reference   B. array copy
    C. half array   D. selected item of array

KEY (CORRECT ANSWERS)

1.	D	11.	A
2.	C	12.	B
3.	C	13.	C
4.	A	14.	A
5.	C	15.	D
6.	B	16.	A
7.	A	17.	C
8.	B	18.	D
9.	A	19.	C
10.	D	20.	D

21. D
22. B
23. D
24. C
25. A

TEST 2

DIRECTIONS: Each question or incomplete statement is followed by several suggested answers or completions. Select the one that BEST answers the question or completes the statement. *PRINT THE LETTER OF THE CORRECT ANSWER IN THE SPACE AT THE RIGHT.*

1. What makes Java "Write Once, Run Anywhere"? 1.____
   A. Binary sequence   B. Mnemonics
   C. CLR   D. Bytecode

2. Java is platform independent. 2.____
   The above statement is
   A. true   B. false   C. partially true   D. unclear

3. An engine that interprets compiled code into machine level code is the 3.____
   A. JRE   B. JVM   C. JDK   D. JMS

4. The command used to get running JVM instance is 4.____
   A. java   B. jjvm   C. javac   D. run

5. The concept of programming in which execution flow is determined by parameter is called a 5.____
   A. loop   B. sequence
   C. decision-making statements   D. assignments

6.
```
public static void main (String[]args){
    int count = 0;
    do {
        count++;
        System.out.println("Hello world");
        ++count;
    } while (count < 10);
}
}
```
   6.____

   What will be the output of the above code?
   "Hello world" prints _____ times.
   A. 4   B. 11   C. 8   D. 9

7. Which one of the following allows uncountable execution paths? 7.____
   A. If else   B. Switch   C. For loop   D. While loop

8. for(;;){ } 8.____
   The above statement is
   A. true   B. false
   C. a runtime error   D. a compile-time error

9.
```
Class Test {
    int a;
    int b;

    void math(int a, int b) {
        a * = 2;
        b / + 2;
    }

    public static void main(String args []){

        Test test = new Test();
        int a = 10
        int b - 20;
        test.math(a , b);
        System.out.println(a + "-" + b);
    }
}
```
What will be the output of the above program?
A. 20 – 10   B. 10 – 20   C. 30 – 20   D. 10 - 30

10.
```
class Test {
    int a;
    int b;

    Test(int a, int b){
        this.a = a;
        this.b = b;
    }

    void calculate(Test test){
        test.a * = 2;
        test.b / = 2;
    }

    public static void main(String args [] {
        Test test = new Test(10,20);
        test.calculate(test);
        System.out.println(test.a + "-" + test.b);
    }
}
```
What will be the output of the above program?
A. 20 – 10   B. 10 – 20   C. 30 – 20   D. 10 - 30

11. ```
    class Overloading Test {
        int x;
        int y;

        void add(int a){
            x = a + 1;
            add(a,x);
        }

        void add(int a, int b){
            x = a + 2;
        }

        public static void main(String args [] {
            Overloading Test test = new Overloading Test();
            test.add(6);
            System.out.println(test.x);
        }
    }
    ```
    What will be the output of the above program?
    A. 6   B. 8   C. 7   D. 10

12. ```
    public class Overloading Test {
        int x;
        int y;

        void addInteger(int x){
            this.x = x + 1;
        }
        void addInteger(int x, int y){
            this.x = x * 2;
        }
        public static void main(String args[] {
            Overloading Test test - new Overloading Test();
            int x = 0;
            test.addInteger(6, 7);
            System.out.println(test.x);
        }
    }
    ```
    What will be the output of the above program?
    A. 9   B. 8   C. 10   D. 12

13. If an array is of size 10 like array[10], then how can the fourth element access?
    A. array[4]   B. array(4)   C. array[3]   D. array(3)

14. In Java, String is a(n)
    A. object   B. literal   C. class   D. interface

15. ```
    public class Test {
        public static void main(String []args){
            String str = new String("Hello");
            if("Hello" == str){
                System.out.println("Equal Values");
            } else {
                System.out.println("Not Equal Values");
            }
        }
    }
    ```
    What will be the output of the above program?
    A. The program will be compiled and print "Equal Values"
    B. The program will be compiled and print "Not Equal Values"
    C. Runtime error: string literals cannot be compared with String object
    D. The program will be compiled with warning "Dead Code" on else block

16. ```
    public class Test {
        public static void main(String []args){
            String str1 = new String("Hello");
            String str2 = new String("Hello");

            if(str1.equals(str2) ) {
                System.out.println("Equal Objects");
            } else {
                System.out.println("Not Equal Objects");
            }
        }
    }
    ```
    What will be the output of the above program?
    A. The program will be compiled and print "Equal Objects"
    B. The program will be compiled and print "Not Equal Objects"
    C. Runtime error: string literals cannot be compared with String object
    D. The program will be compiled with warning "Dead Code" on else block

17. Java does not fully qualify object-oriented methodology due to
    A. global variables   B. constants
    C. loops   D. primitive data types

18. _____ is the process of hiding details of a program that is unnecessary for a user in a particular context.
    A. Encapsulation   B. Abstraction
    C. Information Hiding   D. Data Hiding

19. _____ is the process of bundling different items (like fields and methods) into a single class.
    A. Encapsulation   B. Abstraction
    C. Information Hiding   D. Data Hiding

20. _____ is an ability of a class to get the properties of another class and promote reusability. 20.____
    A. Inheritance	B. Composition
    C. Aggregation	D. Association

21. Which of the following methods is used to get the size of the file in bytes? 21.____
    A. Size()	B. FileLength()	C. GetBytes()	D. Length()

22. _____ method is called to remove files from disk. 22.____
    A. Remove()	B. RemoveTo()
    C. Delete()	D. DeletePermanently()

23. Java provides _____ overloaded constructors to create File object. 23.____
    A. 1	B. 2	C. 3	D. 4

24. _____ method returns an array of files and directories name in the given directory path. 24.____
    A. List()	B. ListFiles()
    C. ListFiles(filter fileFilter)	D. ListRoots

25. Suppose Beta is the child class of Alpha 25.____
    Alpha a = new Alpha();
    Beta b = a;
    Which of the following expressions evaluates to false?
    A. Beta instanceof Alpha	B. Beta instanceof Beta
    C. Alpha instanceof Beta	D. Alpha instanceof Alpha

KEY (CORRECT ANSWERS)

1.	D		11.	B
2.	C		12.	D
3.	B		13.	C
4.	A		14.	C
5.	C		15.	B
6.	A		16.	A
7.	B		17.	D
8.	A		18.	B
9.	B		19.	A
10.	A		20.	A

21. D
22. C
23. D
24. A
25. C

TEST 3

DIRECTIONS: Each question or incomplete statement is followed by several suggested answers or completions. Select the one that BEST answers the question or completes the statement. *PRINT THE LETTER OF THE CORRECT ANSWER IN THE SPACE AT THE RIGHT.*

1. _____ is the ability of the program to handle unexpected conditions.
   A. Simplicity
   B. Robustness
   C. Multithreaded
   D. Scalable

   1.____

2. The syntax error is also called the _____ error.
   A. runtime
   B. logical
   C. stack overflow
   D. compile time

   2.____

3. A type of error not detected by the compiler is the _____ error.
   A. runtime
   B. logical
   C. stack overflow
   D. compile time

   3.____

4. What is the searching and fixing of bugs in a source code called?
   A. Inspection   B. Watching   C. Debugging   D. Repairing

   4.____

5. What happens when the following line of code is executed: for(;;){ }?
   A. Unexpected behavior of program
   B. System goes in infinite loop
   C. "//" prints infinite times
   D. "//" prints one time

   5.____

6.
```
public class Test {
    public static void main(String []args){
        int i = 2;

        switch(i){
            case 1:
            System.out.println(1);
            break;
            case 2:
            System.out.println(2);
            break;
            case 2:
            System.out.println(2);
            break;
        }
    }
}
```
What is the expected output of the above code?
   A. 22
   B. 2
   C. Duplicate case error
   D. Runtime error

   6.____

7. To skip a particular iteration and leave the remaining code execution, which statement is used? 7.____
   A. Continue   B. Break   C. Return   D. Exit

8. Which of the following loops is executed even if the initial condition is false? 8.____
   A. For   B. Do-while   C. While   D. For each

9. Which one of these cases is INVALID for method overloading? 9.____
   A. Methods have same data types, same sequence, and same number of parameters in parameter list.
   B. Methods have different data types but same number of parameters.
   C. Methods have different data types and different number of parameters.
   D. Methods have same data types and different number of parameters.

10. What will happen when the main method is overloaded in class? 10.____
    A. Runtime error   B. Method is overloaded
    C. Exception throws   D. Compile-time error

11.
```
class Test {
    int x;
    int y;

    Test(){
        // write something here
    }
    Test(int x, int y){
        // write something here
    }
    Test(int x){
        // write something here
    }
}
```
11.____

    In reading the above class, what do you understand by the constructors?
    A. It is invalid to define multiple constructors.
    B. Constructors must be in sequence with respect to the number of parameters.
    C. They are overloaded constructors.
    D. Default constructor must be private.

12. The _____ defines what object, method, and variable is visible in other parts of the program. 12.____
    A. scope   B. lifetime   C. modifiers   D. state

13. The _____ method is used to explicitly put a String object in string pool. 13.____
    A. format()   B. ValueOf()   C. intern()   D. toPool()

14. The modification of immutable String object results in
    A. a new object
    B. overriding an existing object
    C. Appending an existing object
    D. Creating a new object and dereferencing the existing object

15. When String is created using string literal, it is created in the
    A. heap   B. stack   C. string pool   D. register

16. When this line will execute: "Hello".compareToIgnoreCase("hEllo)"), what will be the output?
    A. 1   B. 0   C. -1   D. -2

17. _____ is a way of writing general code that can work on multiple types.
    A. Inheritance B. Composition C. Aggregation   D. Polymorphism

18. Instance member marked with _____ cannot be inherited.
    A. protected   B. default   C. private   D. public

19. Which one of the following statements is invalid about "this"?
    A. It is used to invoke current class instance.
    B. It can be used to refer current class object.
    C. It can be used to call current class method and fields.
    D. It can also be used to call static members.

20. _____ keyword is used to call the immediate super class instance, method, and constructor.
    A. Super   B. This   C. SuperClass   D. Strictfp

21. Which of the following constructors is used to initialize an input object for file? Scanner sc = new
    A. Scanner(tmp.txt)   B. Scanner(new File("tmp.txt"))
    C. Scanner("tmp.txt")   D. Scanner(File("tmp.txt"))

22. ```
    class InputOutput {
        public static void main(String []args){
            Scanner sc = new Scanner(System.in);
            inti = sc.nextInt();
            System.out.println(i);
            sc.close();
        }
    }
    ```
    What will be the possible output of the above program when the user enters '21L'?
    A. The code throws runtime exception "InputMismatchException".
    B. 2L, long value is converted into integer and prints 2.
    C. The compiler takes 2L as string and prints '2L'.
    D. The compiler takes 2L as string and skips 'L' prints 2.
    ```

23.
```
class InputOutput {
    public static void main(String []args){
        Scanner sc = new Scanner(System.in);
        Double d1 = sc.nextDouble();
        String line = sc.nextLine();
        Double d2 - sc.nextDouble();
        System.out.println(d1 + " "+d2);
        sc.close();
    }
}
```
What will be the possible output of the above program when the user enters '2' then Press Enter Key then enter '3'?
- A. Program is compiled successfully and prints '2 3'.
- B. Program throws runtime error and cannot convert integer into double.
- C. Program is compiled successfully, and prints '2.0 3.0'.
- D. Program is compiled successfully, and prints '2.0\n3.0'.

24. Scanner class has the _____ method to read a single word.
- A. nextWord()
- B. next()
- C. nextString()
- D. next(String pattern)

25. PrintWriter does not support writing raw bytes on the stream. What is the alternative way of writing bytes?
- A. Use encoded byte stream
- B. Use unencoded byte stream
- C. Use byte array
- D. Use byte wrapper class

KEY (CORRECT ANSWERS)

1.	B		11.	C
2.	D		12.	A
3.	B		13.	C
4.	C		14.	A
5.	B		15.	C
6.	C		16.	C
7.	A		17.	D
8.	B		18.	C
9.	A		19.	D
10.	D		20.	A

21. C
22. A
23. C
24. B
25. B

TEST 4

DIRECTIONS: Each question or incomplete statement is followed by several suggested answers or completions. Select the one that BEST answers the question or completes the statement. *PRINT THE LETTER OF THE CORRECT ANSWER IN THE SPACE AT THE RIGHT.*

1. _____ data type represents indivisible and atomic value.
   A. Object   B. Class   C. Primitive   D. Pointer

2. The data representation component of a data type determines how value is stored in terms of
   A. size of heap
   B. register representation
   C. data size and format
   D. data encoding

3. What is the difference between variables and constants?
   A. Nothing
   B. Constant identifier must be in uppercase
   C. A variable can change its value, whereas constant cannot
   D. A constant can change variable, whereas variable cannot

4. Suppose: inti = 17, j = 0.17;
   If the following line executes "System.out.println(i==j);", then what is the possible outcome?
   A. Compile-time error   B. True
   C. Runtime error   D. False

5. ```
   public class Test {
       public static void main(String []args){
           int sum = 0;

           for (int a = 0, b = 0; a < 5 & b < 5; ++a, b = a + 1){
               sum ++a;
           }
           System.out.println(sum);
       }
   }
   ```
   What is the output of the above code?
   A. 6   B. 14
   C. 5   D. Compile-time error

6. Super class of Exception is
   A. Exception   B. Throwable
   C. RuntimeException   D. IOExce

7. Which block must execute whether exception comes or not?
   A. Start   B. Catch   C. Finally   D. Finalize
   ```

8.
```
class Test{
    public static void main(String[]args){
        try{
            int a = 10/0;
            System.out.print("in try");
            return;
        }catch(Exception e){
            System.out.print("in catch");
            return;
        }finally{
            System.out.print("in finally");
            return;
        }
    }
}
```
What is the output of the above code?
A. In try
B. In try in catch
C. In catch in finally
D. In try in finally

9. The _____ method is used to display detailed exception messages.
A. printStackTrace()
B. getMessage()
C. printExceptionMessage()
D. getException()

10.
```
void checkScope(){
    int a = 0;
    {
        a = 10;
        {
            a = 13;
            {
                a b = a + 14;
            }
        }
        System.out.println(a);
    }
}
```
Considering the above method, what is the expected output of variable 'a'?
A. 0
B. Compile-time error
C. 13
D. Out of Scope Exception

11.
```
void checkScope(){
    int a = 0;
    {
        int b = a + 14;
    }
    System.out.println(b);
}
```
Considering the above method, what is the expected output of variable 'b'?
A. 14
B. 014
C. Compile-time error
D. Runtime error

12. ```
    void checkScope(){
        int a = 1;
        {
            int b = a + 14;
        }
            int b = a + 14;
        }
        int b = 10;
        System.out.println(b);
    }
    ```
    Considering the above method, what will be the expected output?
    A. Compile-time error as b initialized 3 times
    B. Compile-time error as b initialized in both outer and inner scope
    C. Runtime error
    D. Successfully executed as the first two initialized in their own scope and third one initialized at the end

13. A _____ statement returns the control to the caller.
    A. return   B. break   C. continue   D. goto

14. Which of the following is the possible line of code to check string starts with "Good" if string is "Good Morning"?
    A. If (s.startsWith("Good"))
    B. If (s.indexOf("Good") == 1)
    C. If (s.charAt(1) == 'G' && s.charAt(2) == '0' && s.charAt(3) == '0' && s.charAt() == 'd'){
    D. If (s.substring(0,3).equals("Good"))

15. The _____ method is used to convert byte array into a string.
    A. toStringArray()   B. toArrayChar()
    C. toArrayString()   D. toCharArray()

16. Suppose String str = "Good", the method _____ returns a new string "Good".
    A. s.trim(s)   B. String.trim(s)
    C. trim(s)   D. s.trim()

17. Which one of the following statements is CORRECT?
    A. int a = new int(10);
    B. int[] c = {2, 4, 6, 8};
    C. char[] d = new char();
    D. char[] e = new char{'i', 'j', 'k', 'l'}[];
    ```

18.
```
public class Test{
    int num;
    Test(int num){
        ____.num = num;
    }
}
```
Which of the following keywords fills in the blank in the above code?
A. super   B. obj   C. new   D. this

19.
```
class test{
    public static void main(String []args){
        Beta beta = new Beta();
    }
}
class alpha{
    int val = 7;

    public Alpha(){
    printRay();
    System.out.println("In Alpha");
    }
    public void printRay(){
    }
}
class beta extends Alpha{
    public Beta(){
    System.out.println("In Beta");
    }
    public void print Ray(){
    System.out.println("Beta Ray");
    }
}
```
What will be the output of the above code?
 A. First Beta class constructor called Alpha class's constructor and print "Beta Ray" by calling the overridden child method then print "In Alpha" and at last print "In Beta"
 B. First Alpha class constructor called and print "Beta Ray" by calling the overridden child method then print "In Alpha" and at last print "In Beta"
 C. The Alpha class constructor called overridden method and print "Alpha Ray"
 D. The Beta class constructor called and prints "In Beta"

20.
```
public class Test{
    public static void main(String []args){
        Alpha alpha = new Alpha();
        alpha.printRay();
        Beta beta = new Beta();
        beta.printRay();
    }
}
public class Alpha{
    public void printRay(){
        System.out.println(getRay());
    }
    public String getRay(){
        return "Alpha";
    }
}
public class Beta extends Alpha{
    public String getRay(){
        return "Beta";
    }
}
```
What will be the output of the above code?
   A. Alpha Alpha
   B. Alpha Beta
   C. Beta Alpha
   D. Beta Beta

21. What will be the output of the following code, when Beta is the child class of Alpha?
   A. Compile-time error: mismatch type
   B. Alpha a – new Alpha();
   C. Compiled successfully, object b get the reference of object a
   D. Runtime error: mismatch type

22. What will happen when the following line executes and user presses Enter Key?
   A. String line – sc.nextLine();
   B. A blank string is stored in line, and the program is terminated
   C. Space is stored in line, and the program is terminated
   D. Compile-time error because nextLine() does not return anything
   E. Runtime error because nextLine() returns character

23. _____ is an inherited field in the PrintWriter class to synchronize operations on stream.
   A. Synchronized
   B. Sync
   C. Hold
   D. Lock

24. Which one of the following given constructors is used to initialize an output object for file?
    PrintWriter writer = new
    A. PrintWriter(tmp.txt);
    B. PrintWriter(new File("tmp.txt"));
    C. PrintWriter(new file("tmp.txt"));
    D. PrintWriter(file("tmp.txt"));

    24.____

25. PrintWriter has a _____ method to clear the data in buffer.
    A. close()   B. flush()   C. clear()   D. closeflush()

    25.____

KEY (CORRECT ANSWERS)

1.	C	11.	C
2.	C	12.	D
3.	C	13.	A
4.	D	14.	A
5.	A	15.	D
6.	B	16.	D
7.	C	17.	B
8.	C	18.	D
9.	B	19.	A
10.	C	20.	B

21. A
22. B
23. D
24. B
25. B

EXAMINATION SECTION
TEST 1

DIRECTIONS: Each question or incomplete statement is followed by several suggested answers or completions. Select the one that BEST answers the question or completes the statement. *PRINT THE LETTER OF THE CORRECT ANSWER IN THE SPACE AT THE RIGHT.*

1. Users use _____ devices to send instructions to the computer. 1._____
   A. input
   B. output
   C. memory unit
   D. handlers

2. The _____ number system is used to perform arithmetic operations. 2._____
   A. hexadecimal   B. decimal   C. binary   D. octal

3. The CPU executes instructions in _____ cycle. 3._____
   A. save/run
   B. do/destroy
   C. convert/run
   D. fetch/execute

4. The register that holds the address of the currently executing instruction is 4._____
   A. program counter
   B. processor register
   C. bus
   D. instant register

5. A device that is capable of both input and output operations is a _____ device. 5._____
   A. storage   B. output   C. input   D. display

6. An If statement supports expression that evaluate to a(n) _____ data type. 6._____
   A. int   B. boolean   C. char   D. string

7.
```
private void checkIf(){
    boolean x = false;        //Line 1
    if(x=true){               //Line 2
        system,out.prinIn("True");   //Line 3
    }else{
        System.out.printIn("False");
    }
}
```
What will be the output of the above code? 7._____
   A. Syntax error on Line 1
   B. Syntax error on Line 2
   C. True
   D. False

8. A switch statement can evaluate integer data type which includes 8._____
   A. byte, int, long
   B. short, int, byte
   C. long, int, short
   D. char, long, int

9.
```
private void checkSwitch(){
    int a = 2;
    switch (a){
        default:
            a++;
        case 1:
            ++a;
    }
    System.out.println(a);
}
```
What will be the output of the above code?
A. 3
B. 2
C. 4
D. Syntax error, as default block comes before case statement

9._____

10. In switch case, a _____ keyword is used to execute code when none of the cases match with switch condition.
A. default   B. break   C. continue   D. match

10._____

11. When an object variable passes into method, object _____ is passed.
A. copy   B. reference   C. value   D. type

11._____

12. The reference variable holds _____, which is the address of a specific object in the heap.
A. bits
B. string
C. hex code
D. stack pointer

12._____

13. When the object reference passes into a method, a _____ of an object reference is passed. Hence, both (caller and called method) refer to the same object on the heap.
A. value
B. original
C. copy
D. string representation

13._____

14.
```
public class PassByValue Test{
    public static void main (String { [] args){
    int x = 2;

    PassByValueTest passByValue Test = new PassByValueTest();

    System.out.println("Before change(2) x = " + x);
    passByValueTest.change(x);
    System,out,println("After change(1) x = " + x);
    }
    void change(int num){
    num = num + 1;
    System.out.println("changed value = " + num);
    }
}
```

14._____

What will be the output of the above code?
- A. Before change(2) x = 2
  changed value = 3
  After change(2) x = 3
- B. Before change(2) x = 3
  changed value = 2
  After change(2) x = 2
- C. Before change(2) x = 2
  changed value = 2
  After change(2) x = 3
- D. Before change(2) x = 2
  changed value = 3
  After change(2) x = 2

15. ```
    public class PassByRereneTest{
       int num;
       void modifyIt(int num){
          num = num + 200;
          System.out.println("num in modify as" + num);
       }
       public static void main (String [] args) {
       PassByRereneTest passByRereneTest = new PassByRerene Test();
       System.out.println("num = " + 4);
       passByRereneTest.num = 4;
       passByRereneTest.modifyIt(passByRereneTest.num);
       System.out.println("num after modifyIt is " + passByRereneTest.num);
       }
    }
    ```
    What will be the output of the above code?
    - A. num = 4
      num in modify as 204
      num after modifyIt is 4
    - B. num = 4
      num in modify as 204
      num after modifyIt is 204
    - C. num = 4
      num in modifyIt is 204
      num after modifyIt is 204
    - D. num = 4
      num in modify as 4
      num after modifyIt is 4

16. Which of the following is an invalid array declaration or initialization?
    - A. int[] ar = new int[] {1,2,3,4,5};
    - B. int[] ar = new int[5];
    - C. int[5] a = {1,2,3,4,5}
    - D. int[]b = {1,2,3,4,5};

17. ```
    public class ArrayTest{
       public static void main(String[] args){
          char[] letters = {65, 'A', 0101};
          System.out.println((letters[0] == letters[1]) + " " + (letters[0] = = [2]));
       }
    }
    ```
    What will be the output of the above code?
    - A. Compile time error
    - B. true false
    - C. false false
    - D. true true

18. ```
    public class ArrayTest{
        public static void main(String[] args){
            int[][] ab = {{1,2}, {3,4,7}, {5,6}};
            System.out.println(ab.length + " " + ab[1].length);
        }
    }
    ```
    What will be the output of the above code?
    A. Compilation error
    B. Statement ab[1].length throws ArrayIndexOutOfBoundsException
    C. 3 2
    D. 3 3

19. How can an array last index be accessed?
    A. array.length
    B. array.length-1
    C. array.size
    D. array.size-1

20. On what index is array's first element found?
    A. 0   B. 1   C. -1   D. null

21. A(n) _____ is a specification of an object.
    A. aspect   B. interface   C. class   D. enum

22. A(n) _____ of an object is defined by its data.
    A. state   B. behavior   C. operation   D. mode

23. Which one of the following statements is TRUE about encapsulation?
    A. It is a bundling of related data and behavior of an object
    B. It is a process in which data is protected and accessed only from get and set methods
    C. It is a process in which information irrelevant to the user is hidden
    D. It is a process that allows data to be directly accessed

24. The benefit of the _____ method is that it applies additional conditions and formatting before setting data into variable.
    A. local   B. accessor   C. mutator   D. anonymous

25. The process of hiding details that are irrelevant to the user in a specific context is called
    A. encapsulation   B. abstraction   C. inheritance   D. polymorphism
    ```

KEY (CORRECT ANSWERS)

1.	A	11.	B
2.	C	12.	A
3.	D	13.	C
4.	A	14.	D
5.	A	15.	A
6.	B	16.	C
7.	C	17.	D
8.	B	18.	D
9.	C	19.	B
10.	A	20.	A

21.	C
22.	A
23.	B
24.	C
25.	B

TEST 2

DIRECTIONS: Each question or incomplete statement is followed by several suggested answers or completions. Select the one that BEST answers the question or completes the statement. *PRINT THE LETTER OF THE CORRECT ANSWER IN THE SPACE AT THE RIGHT.*

1. Software responsible for executing other software is called a(n)
   A. application software
   B. operating system
   C. utility software
   D. toolkit

   1._____

2. A compiler is a type of _____ software.
   A. translation   B. application   C. operating   D. mixing

   2._____

3. The _____ provides all the capabilities to develop software.
   A. notepad
   B. wordpad
   C. adobe reader
   D. IDE

   3._____

4. Missing parenthesis and delimiters lead to a _____ error.
   A. syntax   B. logical   C. sensible   D. runtime

   4._____

5. The _____ error is the most difficult to identify.
   A. syntax   B. logical   C. compile time   D. runtime

   5._____

6. ```
   private void checkFor(){
       int a = 1;
       for(;a<10;){
           System.out.println(a);
       }
   }
   ```
   What will be the output of the above code?
   A. Error in for loop syntax
   B. Runtime error as increment statement is missing
   C. Code prints 1 to 9 digits
   D. Code prints 1 infinite times

   6._____

7. If a method has a return type 'void,' it means method returns
   A. nothing
   B. null
   C. an empty object
   D. 0

   7._____

8. Which of the following is invalid for a loop statement?
   A. int a=0; for(;a<10-; a++){}
   B. for(int a = 1, b = 2; a < 10; a++){}
   C. for(int a = 1, b = 9; a < 10; a++,b++){}
   D. for(;false;){}

   8._____

9. The _____ statement is used to stop the current iteration of the loop.
   A. continue   B. break   C. return   D. stop

   9._____
   ```

10. Java uses the _____ value of character during comparison.
    A. UTF8 B. UNICODE C. ASCII D. UTF-16

11. Primitive return types do not accept _____ value.
    A. signed B. negative C. character D. null

12. A method whose return type is object reference can return sub type object reference, the returning type is called _____ return.
    A. null B. primitive C. covariant D. shallow

13. Which of the following statements is CORRECT?
    A. It is legal to add an empty return statement in a method whose return type is void
    B. The method having returned type object reference cannot return null
    C. The array is a perfect legal type to declare in method signature only
    D. Overloaded method does not change return type

14. private List check(){
     ArrayList list = new ArrayList();
     list = null   //Line 1
     return list;   //Line 2
    }
    What will be the output of the above code?
    A. The null object of subtype cannot be returned
    B. Compile time error on Line 2; subtype cannot be returned
    C. Program crashes at runtime at Line 1
    D. The method is successfully compiled and executed

15. public class TestReturn {
     public static void main(String{} args){
      TestReturn.emptyReturn(2);
     }
     private static void emptyReturn(int a){
      a + = 10;   //Line 1
      return;   //Line 2
      System.out.println(a); //Line 3
    What will be the output of the above code?
    A. The program is successfully compiled and executed and prints 12
    B. It is illegal to use a return statement in a method whose return type is void
    C. No return value is given at Line 2
    D. Syntax error at Line 3, unreachable code

16. Suppose an int array declare as int[] ar = {}; what will be the result when the following line is executed: System.out.println(ar[0]);?
    A. Program throws NullPointerException
    B. Compile time error
    C. Array's hex code prints
    D. The statement throws ArrayIndexOutOfBoundsException

17. String[] str = new String [4];
    What will be the output by the above statement?
    A. Four String objects created
    B. One String array created with 4 String objects
    C. Only one String array created
    D. It is illegal to create String array

18. ```
    public class ArrayTest{
        public static void main(String[] args)}
            int[] nums = new int[10];
            for(int a = 0, b = 0; a < 20; a++){
                if(a%2 = = 0){
                nums[b] = a;
                ++b;
                }
            }
            for(int a = 0; a < nums.length-1; a++){
                System.out.print(nums[a] + " ");
            }
        }
    }
    ```
    What will be the output of the above code?
    A. 0 2 4 6 8 10 12 14 16   B. 0 2 3 4 8 13
    C. 1 3 5 7 9   D. 1 1 2 3 5 6

19. ```
    public class OverloadTest {
        public static void main(String[] args){
            System.out.println("main 1");
        }
        public static void main(String[] args){
            System.out.println("main 2");
        }
    }
    ```
    What will be the output of the above code?
    A. main 1 main 2
    B. main 1
    C. Compile time error, main method cannot be overloaded
    D. Runtime error

20. Which of the following statements is NOT true for String object?
    A. String object is immutable
    B. String object reference is immutable
    C. String class cannot be extended
    D. String literals store in the pool

21. Class members with _____ modifier are accessible in their own package as well as in derived classes.
    A. default   B. public   C. protected   D. private

22. How does a field make read-only?
    A. By prefixing the field with the read-only keyword
    B. Make mutator method private
    C. Set variable as final
    D. Mark field as static

    22._____

23. A(n) _____ keyword is used to keep the method from overriding.
    A. abstract   B. final   C. static   D. private

    23._____

24. The characteristic of an OOP in which object can refer to one of its derived class is called
    A. generalization   B. aggregation
    C. collection   D. polymorphism

    24._____

25. If a class holds an instance of another class, this relation falls in the _____ concept.
    A. IS-A   B. HAS-A   C. HAVE-A   D. ARE-A

    25._____

KEY (CORRECT ANSWERS)

1.	B		11.	D
2.	A		12.	C
3.	D		13.	A
4.	A		14.	D
5.	B		15.	D
6.	D		16.	D
7.	A		17.	C
8.	D		18.	A
9.	A		19.	C
10.	B		20.	B

21.	C
22.	B
23.	B
24.	D
25.	B

TEST 3

DIRECTIONS: Each question or incomplete statement is followed by several suggested answers or completions. Select the one that BEST answers the question or completes the statement. *PRINT THE LETTER OF THE CORRECT ANSWER IN THE SPACE AT THE RIGHT.*

1. The compiler is unable to identify a _____ error.
   A. syntax
   B. logical
   C. compile time
   D. runtime

2. Long literals postfix with
   A. L
   B. Long
   C. i
   D. Li

3. The _____ datatype supports binary, octal and hexadecimal literals.
   A. short
   B. float
   C. integer
   D. boolean

4. Which one of the statements is CORRECT when initializing boolean?
   boolean b =
   A. 'false'
   B. 0
   C. /1
   D. true

5. What is the CORRECT way to initialize float?
   float f =
   A. 4.0
   B. 4
   C. 4d
   D. 4.0

6. 'operator' _____ the operands if one of the operands is a strong.
   A. add
   B. subtract
   C. convert String into int
   D. concat

7. ```
   private void checkString(){
       String str = "11";    //Line 1
       int num = str + 2     //Line 2
   }
   ```
   What will be the output of the above code?
   A. A type mismatch error occurs on Line 2 at compile time
   B. A type mismatch error occurs on Line 2 at runtime
   C. Variable str auto casts at runtime and added to 2 and set 14 in num
   D. Variable str auto casts at runtime and added to 2 and set 112 in num

8. The _____ operator returns the opposite boolean value of an evaluated expression.
   A. ternary
   B. inversion
   C. rational
   D. increment

9. The occurrence of abnormal condition that alters normal program behavior is called
   A. exception
   B. error
   C. bug
   D. defect
   ```

10. A block of code responsible for handling exception is called
    A. throw block
    B. error handler
    C. exception handler
    D. catch handler

11. The _____ variable is lived until its method is on the stack.
    A. local B. instance C. static D. temporary

12.
```
public class InstanceScope {
    int inst = 1;
    public static void main(String[] args) {
        inst++;                        //Line 1
        {
            int inst = 10;             //Line 2
        }
        System.out.println(inst);      //Line 2
    }
}
```
What will be the output of the above code?
The program will
    A. compile but at runtime crash on Line 1
    B. not compile due to an error on Line 1 and Line 2
    C. not compile due to an error on Line 1 only
    D. successfully compile and run

13. _____ variable is alive until block execution completes.
    A. Block B. Temporary C. Class D. Instance

14. Which of the following statements BEST define overloading?
    A. Overloading is defined as a method having the same name, same parameter type, but the number of parameters is different
    B. Overloading is a re-use of an already defined method name, but different parameter types
    C. The method is called overloaded if its return type must be the same with the already defined method
    D. If a method has the same signature with the already defined method, it is called overloading

15. Suppose there is a method overloadMe and it is defined as:
    void overloadMe(float f, String s) throws MalformedInput Exception {}
    Which one of the following declarations does NOT comply with overloading rules and gets an error?
    A. void overloadMe(String s, float f) throws NumberFormatException {}
    B. void overloadMe(float f, String s) throws NumberFormatException {}
    C. int overloadMe(double f, String s) throws IOException {return 0;}
    D. void overloadMe(char ch) throws ArrayIndexOutOfBoundsException {}

16. ```
    public class StringTest {
        public static void main(String{} args) {
            String str = "s";
            if(str.startsWith("s"))
                str + = "art";
            if(str = = "starts")
                str + = "true";
            System.out.println(str);
        }
    }
    ```
    What will be the output of the above code?
    A. start   B. true   C. starttrue   C. strue

17. ```
    public class StringTest {
        public static void main(String[] args) }
            String[] sArray = {"day", "weekday", "month");
            for(int i  = 1; i < sArray.length-1; i++) {
                System.out.println(sArray[i].toUpperCase());
            }
        }
    }
    ```
    What will be the output of the above code?
    A. WEEKDAYMONTH   B. DAYWEEKDAY
    C. WEEKDAY   D. MONTH

18. Which of the methods is used to get the single character from string on giving index?
    A. substring()   B. charAt()   C. chatAT()   D. get()

19. ```
    public class StringTest {
        public static void main(String[] args) {
            String str = "Map";
            int i = 1;
            System.out.println(str + = i);
        }
    }
    ```
    What will be the output of the above code?
    A. Compile time error   B. Runtime error
    C. Map1   D. 1Map1

20. ```
    public class StringTest {
        public static void main(String[] args) {
            String s1 = "abc", s2 = "abc";
            String s3 = new String("abc");
            String s4 = new String("abc");
            System.out.print(s1 = = s2);
            System.out.print(s3 = = s4);
        }
    }
    ```

What will be the output of the above code?
A. true false   B. false false   C. true true   D. false true

21. In inheritance, members with _____ modifiers cannot be inherited.   21._____
    A. public   B. protected   C. default   D. private

22. A method that is used to initialize object state is called a   22._____
    A. method   B. field   C. constructor   D. destructor

23. public class A {   23._____
        public A(){
        system.out.print("inside A");
        }
    }
    public class B extends A {
        public B(){
        System.out.println("inside B");
        }
    }
    public class TestConstructorCalling {
        public static void main(String[] args) {
        A b = new B();
        }
    }
    What will be the output of the above code?
    A. inside A inside B   B. inside B inside A
    C. inside A   D. inside B

24. With reference to the above class TestConstructorCalling, class B called its   24._____
    super class A constructor when its object is initialized. This process is called
    A. calling parent constructor   B. constructor queue
    C. constructor chaining   D. invoking parent

25. A(n) _____ class has a constructor, but it cannot be instantiated.   25._____
    A. abstract   B. concrete   C. enum   D. aspect

KEY (CORRECT ANSWERS)

1. B
2. A
3. C
4. D
5. B

6. D
7. A
8. B
9. A
10. C

11. A
12. B
13. A
14. B
15. B

16. A
17. C
18. B
19. C
20. A

21. D
22. C
23. A
24. C
25. A

TEST 4

DIRECTIONS: Each question or incomplete statement is followed by several suggested answers or completions. Select the one that BEST answers the question or completes the statement. *PRINT THE LETTER OF THE CORRECT ANSWER IN THE SPACE AT THE RIGHT.*

1. The effect of reusing a variable that is already declared is called
   A. reusability B. accessing C. shadowing D. reinitializing

   1.____

2.  ```
    void check(){
        int a = 10;          //Line 1
        float f = 0f;        //Line 2
        short s = 327687     //Line 3
        char c = 'a';        //Line 4
    }
    ```
    In checking out the above function, which line shows a syntax error?
    A. 1 B. 2 C. 3 D. 4

    2.____

3. When creating an object using the syntax (Object obj = new Object();), what does JVM do?
   A. Declare a reference variable obj
   B. Create an object on the stack
   C. Declare and assign reference
   D. Make a reference, create a new object, and assign a reference to obj

   3.____

4. Which of the following is the correct way to assign octal value to int?
   int i =
   A. 01 B. 0X1 C. OCT1 D. 1O

   4.____

5. What will happen when the following statement executes?
   Object obj = null;
   A. Creates an object that holds a null constant
   B. Creates space for obj reference variable
   C. Initializes object with null value
   D. Initializes object with general type

   5.____
    ```

6.
```
private static void checkDoWhile(){
    int a = 2, b = 1;
    String s = " ";

    do{
        switch(a){
        case 3:
            s + = a;
            break;
        case 5:
            s.concat("Hello");
        case 7:
            s + = " "+ a;
        }
        ++a;
        b++;
    }while(b<10);
    System.out.println(s);
}
```
What will be the result of variable 's' when following the executed code?
A. 3 5 7
B. 5 8 Hello
C. Hello 1 2 3
D. 1 3 5 Hello 9

6._____

7.
```
private void checkTryCatch(String b){
    try {
        b + = "try block";
        char c = b.charAt(5);
    } catch (IndexOutOfBoundsException e) {
        b.concat("-exception caught. " + e.getMessage());
        return;
    }finally{
        b.concat("-Ah finally in finally block");
    }
    System.out.println(b);
}
```
What will be the output when the above method executes with argument "Inside"?
A. Inside try block
B. Inside try block – exception caught.IndexOutOfBoundsException
C. Try block – Ah finally in finally block
D. Try block – exception – Ah finally in finally block

7._____

8. Which of the following is the CORRECT while loop expression?
A. int a = 0; while(a){}   B. while("true"){}
C. while(1){}   D. while(false){}

8._____

9.  ```
    public static void ternaryTest(){
        float a = 14.0f;
        String s = (a < 10)? "happy":a > 15)?"world":"today";
        System.out.println(s);
    }
    ```
    What will be the output of the above code?
    A. happy
    B. world
    C. today
    D. It is illegal to compare a float with an int

10. The _____ clause is used to tell the JVM what action takes when exception throws.
    A. try   B. finally   C. threw   D. catch

11. The only condition when the finally block does not invoke is when
    A. the JVM executes system.exit() statement
    B. return statement executes in try block
    C. break statement executes in try block
    D. catch block throws an exception

12. The compiler enforces _____ exception to be handled.
    A. runtime   B. checked   C. unchecked   D. compiler

13. _____ is the superclass of all exceptions and returns.
    A. Throwable   B. Error
    C. JVM Exception   D. Defecto

14. What exception will throw when the following line of code is executed?
    Float f = new Float("abc");
    A. IllegalInputStatement   B. NumberCastException
    C. NumberFormatException   D. ClassCastException

15. To call a superclass overridden method, _____ keyword is used.
    A. this   B. super   C. abstract   D. final

16. ```
    public interface TestInterface {
        public abstract void implementMe(int i);
    }
    ```
    What will be the CORRECT class definition when it implements the above interface?
    A. abstract class IClass implements TestInterface{}
    B. class IClass extends TestInterface{
         public void implementMe(){}
       }

C. ```
class IClass implements TestInterface {
    public void implementMe(String s) {}
}
```
D. ```
class IClass implements TestInterface {
    public abstract void implementMe(int i);
}
```

17. Every object of class has its own copy of _____ method.
    A. static   B. local   C. instance   D. final

18. ```
    public class B {
        static int a;
        int x;
        static void show(){
            x = 9;        //Line 1
        }
        void print(){
            a = 10;       //Line 2
        }
    }
    ```
    What will happen when the above program is compiled?
    A. Compile time error at Line 1
    B. Compile time error at Line 2
    C. Compile time error at both Line 1 and Line 2
    D. No compile time error

19. ```
    public class Animal{
        public void getSound(){
        System.out.print("animal sound-");
        }
    }
    class Dog extends Animal{
        public void getSound(){
        super.getSound();
        System.out.print("barked");
        }
    }
    class Cat extends Animal{
        public void getSound(){
        super.getSound();
        System.out.print("meow");
        }
    }
    ```

```
class TestAnimal{
    public static void main(String[] args)}
    Animal an = new dog();
    an.getSound();
    an – new Cat();
    an.getSound();
    }
}
```
What will be the output of the above code?
A. barked meow
B. barked barked
C. animal sound – barked animal sound – meow
D. barked animal sound - meow

20. A _____ object represents existing file or directory. 20.____
    A. File   B. Directory   C. FileInstance   D. SystemFile

21. The IO related files are found in _____ package. 21.____
    A. Java.net   B. Java.io
    C. Java.inputoutput   D. Javax.io

22. Which one of the following is NOT a member of Java.io package? 22.____
    A. Writer   B. Reader
    C. ObjectInput   D. DirectoryFilter

23.
```
public class OverloadTest{
    public static void main(String[] args){
        overloadMe(40.4f);                    //Line 1
        overloadMe(40);                       //Line 2
        overloadMe("Method Overloaded");      //Line 3
    }
    static void overloadMe(String s){
        System.out.println(s);
    }
    static void overloadMe(float f){
        System.out.println(f);
    }
}
```
23.____

What will be the output of the above code?
A. Syntax error at Line 2, no overloaded method defines for an int type parameter
B. 40.4
   40
   Method Overloaded
C. 40.4
   Method Overloaded
D. 40.4
   40.0
   Method Overloaded

24.
```
public class OverloadTest{
    public static void main(String[] args){
        overloadMe(40.4);
    }
    static void overloadMe(int i){
        System.out.print(i);
    }
    static void overloadMe(float f){
        System.out.print(f);
    }
}
```
What will be the output of the above code?
A. Compile time error
B. Runtime error
C. 40
D. 40 40.4

24.____

25.
```
public class OverloadTest{
    public static void main(String[] args){
        int a = overloadMe(40);
    }
    static int overloadMe(int i){
        System.out.println(i);
        return i;
    }
    static float overloadMe(int i){
        System.out.println(i);
        return i;
    }
}
```
What will be the output of the above code?
A. 40 40
B. 40
C. Compile time error
D. Runtime error

25.____

KEY (CORRECT ANSWERS)

1.	C	11.	A
2.	C	12.	B
3.	D	13.	A
4.	A	14.	C
5.	B	15.	B
6.	A	16.	A
7.	A	17.	C
8.	D	18.	A
9.	C	19.	C
10.	D	20.	A

21.	B
22.	D
23.	D
24.	A
25.	C

GLOSSARY OF COMPUTER TERMS

Basic

accessibility
The term accessibility refers to information that can be accessed with fewer or no obstacles for as many people as possible. Developers use accessibility features in websites and software to benefit users with disabilities to use computers through assistive technologies.

artificial intelligence
Artificial intelligence or AI is the ability of a computer to perform tasks related to intelligence and think like humans. This technology can process large amounts of data to recognize patterns and make decisions like humans, as seen in programs like ChatGPT.

API
Also called application programming interface, API is a set of protocols and instructions (written in C++ or JavaScript) to determine how two software components will communicate with each other. It defines the kinds of calls and requests made to locate and retrieve the requested information.

application (app)
An application (often called "app" for short) is a computer program that performs specific functions for an end user or another application (in some cases).

authentication
The process of verification of a user or device before allowing access to the system or resources.

bandwidth
A measurement of the amount of data that can be transmitted over a communications path in a given time. The higher the bandwidth, the greater the volume of data transmitted. It is usually measured in bits per second (bps). Modern networks have speed that is measured in the millions of bits per second (megabits per second, or Mbps) or billions of bits per second (gigabits per second, or Gbps).

blockchain
Blockchain technology is an advanced database mechanism that enables the secure sharing of information. It is also known as distributed ledger technology or DLT. The data is stored in blocks that are lined together in a chain.

boot
Starting up an OS is booting it. If the computer is already running, it is more often called rebooting.

browser
A browser is a program used to browse the web. Some common browsers include Google Chrome, Microsoft Edge, Mozilla Firefox, Brave and Safari.

bug
A bug is a mistake in the design of something, especially software. A really severe bug can cause something to crash.

BYOD
Bring Your Own Device or BYOD is a business policy allowing employees to bring in their personal devices and use them to access company data, e-mail and other resources.

Business Intelligence
Business intelligence or BI is a tool that is used by businesses for data collection, analysis and presentation in a meaningful way to drive the decision-making process.

CAPTCHA
Acronym for Completely Automated Public Turing test to tell Computers and Humans Apart. It is

a test in form of distorted text or images that determines if an online user is really a human or an automated user.

cache
A software or hardware component that temporarily stores data in a computing environment to reduce the data retrieval time for future requests.

chatbot
A chat bot or chatterbox is a computer program that is used for simulating and processing human conversation. It is a form of artificial intelligence (AI) that allows humans to interact with digital devices as if they were communicating with a real person.

chat
Chatting is like e-mail, only it is done instantaneously and can directly involve multiple people at once. Chat is a kind of communication over the Internet that allows real-time transmission of messages between sender and receiver. Chat messages are short to enable the participants to respond quickly.

click
To press a mouse button. When done twice in rapid succession, it is referred to as a double-click.

cloud computing
Refers to storage and access data and programs over the Internet instead of any hard drive. Some common cloud services include Dropbox, iCloud and Google Cloud.

cookie
A piece of data from a website stored within a web browser that a website can retrieve at a later time. It is used throughout a user's session to keep track of usage patterns and preferences.

cursor
A point of attention on the computer screen, often marked with a flashing line or block. Text typed into the computer will usually appear at the cursor.

cybercrime
An illegal activity that involves a network or computer. Some common cybercrimes include identity theft, gaining unauthorized access and network intrusions.

cybersecurity
Measures that are designed to protect information, computer devices or networks from cybercrime.

cyberspace
The world of virtual computers, specifically electronic media, used to facilitate online communication.

data center
A physical facility that is used to house an organization's applications and data. The key components of a data center design include servers, storage systems, firewalls, routers, switches and application-delivery controllers.

database
A database is a collection of data, typically organized to make common retrievals easy and efficient. Some common database programs include Oracle, Sybase, Postgres, Mango DB, Microsoft SQL Server, Redis, Filemaker, Adabas, etc.

decryption
It is the process of converting an encrypted message back to its original form. It is the reverse process of encryption.

desktop
A desktop system is a computer designed to sit in one position on a desk somewhere and not move around. Most general-purpose computers are desktop systems. Calling a system a desktop implies nothing about its platform. Industrial desktop systems are typically called workstations.

directory
Also called "folder," a directory is a collection of files typically created for organizational

purposes. Note that a directory is itself a file, so a directory can generally contain other directories. It differs in this way from a partition.

disk
A disk is a physical object used for storing data. It will not forget its data when it loses power. It is always used in conjunction with a disk drive. Some disks can be removed from their drives, some cannot. Generally it is possible to write new information to a disk in addition to reading data from it, but this is not always the case.

drive
A device for storing and/or retrieving data. Some drives (such as disk drives, zip drives, and tape drives) are typically capable of having new data written to them, but some others (like CD-ROMs or DVD-ROMs) are not. Some drives have random access (like disk drives, zip drives, CD-ROMs, and DVD-ROMs), while others only have sequential access (like tape drives).

e-book
An e-book or electronic book is a digital and non-editable text that is available and displayed on electronic devices (smartphone or tablets). The concept behind an e-book is that it should provide all the functionality of an ordinary book but in a manner that is (overall) less expensive and more environmentally friendly. The actual term e-book is somewhat confusingly used to refer to a variety of things: custom software to play e-book titles, dedicated hardware to play e-book titles, and the e-book titles themselves. Individual e-book titles can be free or commercial (but will always be less expensive than their printed counterparts) and have to be loaded into a player to be read. Players vary wildly in capability level. Basic ones allow simple reading and bookmarking; better ones include various features like hypertext, illustrations, audio, and even limited video. Other optional features allow the user to mark-up sections of text, leave notes, circle or diagram things, highlight passages, program or customize settings, and even use interactive fiction.

email
Email is short for electronic mail. It allows for the transfer of information from one user to others, provided they are hooked up via some sort of network Popular email platforms include Gmail and Yahoo.

encryption
The process of data conversion from readable form into encoded form is called encryption. It is used to hide sensitive information and prevent unauthorized access.

end point
Physical devices that are connected to a computer network such as servers, mobile devices, desktop computers and virtual machines.

end user
An individual who will ultimately use an IT product or service.

file
A file is a unit of (usually named) information stored on a computer.

firewall
A network security device that acts as a barrier to monitor and filter incoming and outgoing network traffic and permits/blocks data packets based on previously established security policies.

firmware
Sort of in-between hardware and software, firmware consists of modifiable programs embedded in hardware. Firmware updates should be treated with care since they can literally destroy the underlying hardware if done improperly. There are also cases where neglecting to apply a firmware update can destroy the underlying hardware, so user beware. Cameras, optical drives, printers, mobile phones, network cards, etc. rely on firmware built into their memory for smooth functioning.

floppy
A once-common type of removable disk. Floppy disks did not hold much data, but most

computers were capable of reading them. They typically held 100 KB to 1.44 MB of data.
format
The manner in which data is stored; its organization. For example, VHS, SVHS, and Beta are three different formats of video tape. They are not 100% compatible with each other, but information can be transferred from one to the other with the proper equipment (but not always without loss; SVHS contains more information than either of the other two). Computer information can be stored in literally hundreds of different formats, and can represent text, sounds, graphics, animations, etc. Computer information can be exchanged via different computer types provided both computers can interpret the format used.
freeware
A type of proprietary software that is available for downloading without charge. Depending on the freeware's copyright, the user may or may not reuse the software.
function keys
On a computer keyboard, the keys that start with an "F" and usually (but not always) found on the top row. They are meant to perform user-defined tasks.
GPS
GPS or Global Positioning System is a radio-based global navigation satellite system that allows the user to determine a location on Earth.
graphics
Anything visually displayed on a computer that is not text.
GUI
A graphical user interface (GUI) is a digital interface through which a user interacts with electronic devices (smartphones, computers) with graphical components such as icons, menus, buttons and other visual indicators. GUI representations are manipulated by mouse, touch screen, finger, stylus, or trackball.
hardware
The physical portion of the computer.
help desk
A help desk is an information and assistance resource that provides technical support for hardware or software. Companies provide help desk support to their customers via a toll-free number, e-mail or website. The goal of a help desk is to help customers troubleshoot issues and guide them to navigate technology properly.
hypertext
A hypertext document is like a text document with the ability to contain pointers to other regions of (possibly other) hypertext documents.
IaaS
Infrastructure as a Service (IaaS) is the most basic cloud-service model that offers computing, storage and networking resources on demand and pay-as-you-go basis.
Internet
The Internet is the world-wide network of computers.
IoT
Internet of Things (IoT) refers to the collective network of connected devices and the technology that facilitates communication between devices and the cloud. IoT includes anything with a sensor that is assigned a unique identifier (UID).
IT infrastructure
Systems that are put in place to facilitate operation and management of IT services and environments. There are two types of IT infrastructure: traditional infrastructure and cloud infrastructure.
keyboard
A keyboard on a computer is almost identical to a keyboard on a typewriter. Computer keyboards will typically have extra keys, however. Some of these keys (common examples include Control, Alt, and Fn) are meant to be used in conjunction with other keys just like shift on

a regular typewriter. Other keys (common examples include Insert, Delete, Home, End, Help, function keys,etc.) are meant to be used independently and often perform editing tasks. Keyboards on different platforms will often look slightly different and have somewhat different collections of keys.

LAN
A local area network (LAN) is a group of connected computing devices that usually share a centralized Internet connection. A LAN may serve 2-3 users in a home or thousands of users in a central office.

language
Computer programs can be written in a variety of different languages. Different languages are optimized for different tasks. Common languages include JavaScript, Python, C#, Rust, Kotlin, Swift, Go and Elixir. Some people classify languages into two categories, higher-level and lower-level. These people would consider assembly language and machine language lower-level languages and all other languages higher-level. In general, higher-level languages can be either interpreted or compiled; many languages allow both, but some are restricted to one or the other. Many people do not consider machine language and assembly language at all when talking about programming languages.

laptop
A laptop is any computer designed for portability with the capability to do most of the same functions as a desktop system. They are battery-powered and typically provide several hours of use between charges. Most laptops run Windows or Apple operating systems, though Google's Chromebook laptop has gained in popularity.

learning management system (LMS)
Software that is developed to create, use, manage, deliver and store online training course content for audience. The primary purpose of an LMS is to simplify the learning process for the organization and keep the knowledge of an audience up to date.

machine learning (ML)
A branch of artificial intelligence (AI) that uses data and algorithms to improve the performance of AI to imitate intelligent human behavior.

malware
Malware, also referred to as malicious software, is a program or file that is designed to disrupt computer systems, networks or servers. Some common types of malware include viruses, worms, Trojan horses, ransomware and spyware.

mail server
A mail server is a dedicated software program that supports electronic mail. It stores incoming mail for distribution to users and forwards outgoing mail. Some common mail servers include Microsoft Exchange, iCloud Mail and Sendmail.

memory
Computer memory is used to temporarily store data. In reality, computer memory is only capable of remembering sequences of zeros and ones, but by utilizing the binary number system it is possible to produce arbitrary rational numbers and through clever formatting all manner of representations of pictures, sounds, and animations. The most common types of memory are RAM, ROM, and flash.

MHz & megahertz
One megahertz is equivalent to 1000 kilohertz, or 1,000,000 hertz. The clock speed of the main processor of many computers is measured in MHz, and is sometimes (quite misleadingly) used to represent the overall speed of a computer. In fact, a computer's speed is based upon many factors, and since MHz only reveals how many clock cycles the main processor has per second (saying nothing about how much is actually accomplished per cycle), it can really only accurately be used to gauge two computers with the same generation and family of processor plus similar configurations of memory, co-processors, and other peripheral hardware.

modem
A modem allows two computers to communicate over ordinary phone lines. It derives its name from modulate / demodulate, the process by which it converts digital computer data back and forth for use with an analog phone line.

monitor
The screen for viewing computer information is called a monitor.

mouse
In computer parlance a mouse can be both the physical object moved around to control a pointer on the screen, and the pointer itself.

multimedia
This originally indicated a capability to work with and integrate various types of things including audio, still graphics, and especially video. Now it is more of a marketing term and has little real meaning.

NC
The term network computer refers to any (usually desktop) computer system that is designed to work as part of a network rather than as a stand-alone machine. This saves money on hardware, software, and maintenance by taking advantage of facilities already available on the network. The term "Internet appliance" is often used interchangeably with NC.

network
A network (as applied to computers) typically means a group of computers working together. It can also refer to the physical wires connecting the computers.

notebook
A notebook is a small laptop with similar price, performance, and battery life.

organizer
An organizer is a tiny computer used primarily to store names, addresses, phone numbers, and date book information. They usually have some ability to exchange information with desktop systems. They are extremely inexpensive but are typically incapable of running any special-purpose applications and are thus of limited use.

OS (Operating System)
The operating system is the program that manages a computer's resources. Commonly used OSs include Ubuntu, Windows, MacOS, Android, and Google ChromeOS.

PaaS
Platform as a Service (PaaS) is a cloud computing model that provides a computing platform including hardware, software, and infrastructure for development, running and management of applications. PaaS frees the developers to install in-house hardware and software to develop or run a new application.

PC
The term personal computer properly refers to any desktop, laptop, or notebook computer system. Its use is inconsistent, though, and some use it to specifically refer Windows-based computers.

PDA
A personal digital assistant is a predecessor of mobile phones and smartphones. It is a small battery-powered computer intended to be carried around by the user rather than left on a desk. It is used to carry out certain functions, including scheduling, organization, translation, etc. PDAs largely became obsolete with the advance and improvement of mobile-phone technology.

phishing
A common type of cyberattack that targets victims through phone calls, email, text messages or other forms of communication. This attack aims to trick the receiver by posing as a trustworthy entity to obtain sensitive information such as credit card details, personally identifiable information and login credentials.

platform
Roughly speaking, a platform represents a computer's family. It is defined by both the processor

type on the hardware side and the OS type on the software side. Computers belonging to different platforms cannot typically run each other's programs (unless the programs are written in a language like Java).

portable
If something is portable it can be easily moved from one type of computer to another. The verb "to port" indicates the moving itself.

printer
A printer is a piece of hardware that will print computer information onto paper.

processor
The processor (also called central processing unit, or CPU) is the part of the computer that actually works with the data and runs the programs. There are two main processor types in common usage today: CISC and RISC. Some computers have more than one processor and are thus called "multiprocessor". This is distinct from multitasking. Advertisers often use megahertz numbers as a means of showing a processor's speed. This is often extremely misleading; megahertz numbers are more or less meaningless when compared across different types of processors.

program
A program is a series of instructions for a computer, telling it what to do or how to behave. The terms "application" and "app" mean almost the same thing (albeit applications generally have GUIs). It is however different from an applet. Program is also the verb that means to create a program, and a programmer is one who programs.

run
Running a program is how it is made to do something. The term "execute" means the same thing.

SaaS
Software as a Service (SaaS) is a cloud-based software delivery model that delivers applications over the Internet. SaaS enables companies to use software on-promise without worrying about installing, renewing and maintaining them.

search engine
A software program or tool that enables the users to search information on the internet. It creates indexes of databases based on titles of files, keywords or full text of files. Google, Baidu and Yahoo are some popular search engines.

SEO
SEO or search engine optimization is the process and practice of improving various aspects of a website to increase its visibility in search engines.

software
The non-physical portion of the computer; the part that exists only as data; the programs. Another term meaning much the same is "code."

spam
Use of electronic messaging systems to send unwanted bulk messages. Different types of spam include phishing emails, email spoofing, tech support scams, malspam, spam calls and spam texts.

spreadsheet
A program used to perform various calculations. It is especially popular for financial applications. Some common spreadsheets include Microsoft Excel and Google Sheets.

Trojan horse
A Trojan horse or Trojan is a type of malware that is designed to disguise itself as legitimate code to perform harmful acts. Once it is inside the network, the attacker can carry out any action that legitimate user could perform such as deleting files, modifying data, exporting files, etc.

troubleshooting
The process of providing technical support that includes identification, planning and resolution of problems, faults or errors within the computer system or software.

user
The operator of a computer.

virtual machine
A virtual machine or VM is a computer resource that is not physical. It uses software instead of a physical computer for running programs and deploying applications. VM software can run operating systems, connect to networks, store data and perform other computational functions. Some popular VM include VMware Workstation, VirtualBox, QEMU, Citrix and VMWare Fusion.

VPN
A virtual private network (VPN) is an encrypted internet connection. A VPN hides actual public IP addresses of the user and tunnels the traffic between user's device and the remote server. The aim of using VPN is to ensure sensitive data is safely transmitted.

WAN
A wide area network or WAN is a type of network that exists over a large geographical area.

Wi-Fi
A wireless technology using radio waves to provide high-speed Internet access.

word processor
A program designed to help with the production of textual documents, like letters and memos. Heavier duty work can be done with a desktop publisher. Some common word processors include Microsoft Word and Google Docs.

workstation
A workstation is an individual computer or group of computers that are used by a single user to accomplish professional tasks. Workstations are useful for development and applications that need moderate amount of computing power and high-quality graphics.

www
The World-Wide-Web refers more or less to all the publicly accessible documents on the Internet. It is used quite loosely, and sometimes indicates only HTML files and sometimes FTP and Gopher files, too. It is also sometimes just referred to as "the web".

Reference

The following are past and present elements of computing and computer systems, to be reviewed for reference purposes. In some cases, the element is no longer relevant to modern computing but is important for the study and understanding of previous computing environments.

a11y
Commonly used to abbreviate the word "accessibility." There are eleven letters between the "a" and the "y".

ADA
An object-oriented language at one point popular for military and some academic software.

AIX
The industrial strength OS designed by IBM to run on PowerPC and x86 based machines. It was a variant of UNIX and was meant to provide more power than OS/2.

AJaX
AJaX is a little like DHTML, but it adds asynchronous communication between the browser and Web site via either XML or JSON to achieve performance that often rivals desktop applications.

AltiVec
AltiVec (also called the "Velocity Engine") was a special extension built into some PowerPC CPUs to provide better performance for certain operations, most notably graphics and sound. It was similar to MMX on the x86 CPUs. Like MMX, it required special software for full performance benefits to be realized.

Amiga
A platform originally created and only produced by Commodore and later owned by Gateway 2000 and produced by it and a few smaller companies. It was historically the first multimedia machine and gave the world of computing many innovations. Many music videos were created on Amigas, and a few television series and movies had their special effects generated on Amigas. Also, Amigas were readily synchronized with video cameras, so typically when a computer screen appears on television or in a movie and it is not flickering wildly, it is probably an Amiga in disguise. Many coin-operated arcade games were really Amigas packaged in stand-up boxes.

AmigaOS
The OS used by Amigas. AmigaOS combined the functionality of an OS and a window manager and was fully multitasking. AmigaOS boasted a pretty good selection of games (many arcade games are in fact written on Amigas) but had limited driver support. AmigaOS ran on 68xx, Alpha, and PowerPC based machines.

Apple II
The Apple II computer sold millions of units and is generally considered to have been the first home computer with a 1977 release date. It is based on the 65xx family of processors. The earlier Apple I was only available as a build-it-yourself kit.

AppleScript
A scripting language for Mac OS computers. It is used for basic calculations, text processing and processing complex tasks.

applet
An applet differs from an application in that is not meant to be run stand-alone but rather with the assistance of another program, usually a browser.

Aqua
The default window manager for Mac OS X.

Archie
Archie was a system for searching through FTP archives for particular files. It tends not to be used too much anymore as more general modern search engines are significantly more capable.

ARM
An ARM is a RISC processor invented by Advanced RISC Machines. ARMs are different from most other processors in that they were not designed to maximize speed but rather to maximize speed per power consumed. Thus ARMs found most of their use on hand-held machines and PDAs. A few different OSes run on ARM based machines including Newton OS, JavaOS, Windows CE and Linux. The Cortex-X4 is the fastest ARM CPU ever built.

ASCII
The ASCII character set is the most popular one in common use. People will often refer to a bare text file without complicated embedded format instructions as an ASCII file, and such files can usually be transferred from one computer system to another with relative ease. Unfortunately, there are a few minor variations of it that pop up here and there, and if you receive a text file that seems subtly messed up with punctuation marks altered or upper and lower case reversed, you are probably encountering one of the ASCII variants. It is usually fairly straightforward to translate from one ASCII variant to another, though. The ASCII character set is seven bit while pure binary is usually eight bit, so transferring a binary file through ASCII channels will result in corruption and loss of data. Note also that the ASCII character set is a subset of the Unicode character set.

ASK
A protocol for an infrared communications port on a device. It predates the IrDA compliant infrared communications protocol and is not compatible with it. Many devices with infrared communications support both, but some only support one or the other.

assembly language
Assembly language is essentially machine language that has had some of the numbers

replaced by somewhat easier to remember mnemonics in an attempt to make it more human-readable. The program that converts assembly language to machine language is called an assembler. While assembly language predates FORTRAN, it is not typically what people think of when they discuss computer languages.

authoring system
Any GUIs method of designing new software can be called an authoring system. Any computer language name with the word "visual" in front of it is probably a version of that language built with some authoring system capabilities.

AWK
AWK is an interpreted language developed in 1977 by Aho, Weinberger, & Kernighan. It gets its name from its creators' initials. It was not particularly fast, but it was designed for creating small throwaway programs rather than full-blown applications -- it is designed to make the writing of the program fast, not the program itself. It was quite portable with versions existing for numerous platforms, including a free GNU version. Plus, virtually every version of UNIX in the world came with AWK built-in.

BASIC
The Beginners' All-purpose Symbolic Instruction Code is a computer language developed by Kemeny & Kurtz in 1964.

baud
A measure of communications speed, used typically for modems indicating how many bits per second can be transmitted.

BBS
A bulletin board system was a computer that could be directly connected to via modem and provided various services like e-mail, chatting, newsgroups, and file downloading. BBSs waned in popularity with the rise of Internet access.

BeOS
A lightweight OS available for both PowerPC and x86 based machines. It is often referred to simply as "Be".

beta
A beta version of something is not yet ready for prime time but still possibly useful to related developers and other interested parties. Expect beta software to crash more than properly released software does. Traditionally beta versions (of commercial software) are distributed only to selected testers who are often then given a discount on the proper version after its release in exchange for their testing work. Beta versions of non-commercial software are more often freely available to anyone who has an interest.

binary
There are two meanings for binary in common computer usage. The first is the name of the number system in which there are only zeros and ones. This is important to computers because all computer data is ultimately a series of zeros and ones, and thus can be represented by binary numbers. The second is an offshoot of the first; data that is not meant to be interpreted through a common character set (like ASCII) is typically referred to as binary data. Pure binary data is typically eight bit data, and transferring a binary file through ASCII channels without prior modification will result in corruption and loss of data. Binary data can be turned into ASCII data via uucoding or bcoding.

bit
A bit can either be on or off; one or zero. All computer data can ultimately be reduced to a series of bits. The term is also used as a (very rough) measure of sound quality, color quality, and even processor capability by considering the fact that series of bits can represent binary numbers. For example (without getting too technical), an eight bit image can contain at most 256 distinct colors while a sixteen bit image can contain at most 65,536 distinct colors.

bitmap
A bitmap is a simplistic representation of an image on a computer, simply indicating whether or

not pixels are on or off, and sometimes indicating their color. Often fonts are represented as bitmaps. The term "pixmap" is sometimes used similarly; typically when a distinction is made, pixmap refers to color images and bitmap refers to monochrome images.

blog
Short for web log, a blog is a website or page containing periodic (usually frequent) posts. Blogs are usually syndicated via either some type of RSS or Atom and often supports TrackBacks. It is not uncommon for blogs to function much like newspaper columns. A blogger is someone who writes for and maintains a blog.

boolean
Boolean algebra is the mathematics of base two numbers. Since base two numbers have only two values, zero and one, there is a good analogy between base two numbers and the logical values "true" & "false". In common usage, booleans are therefore considered to be simple logical values like true & false and the operations that relate them, most typically "and", "or" and "not". Since everyone has a basic understanding of the concepts of true & false and basic conjunctions, everyone also has a basic understanding of boolean concepts -- they just may not realize it.

byte
A byte is a grouping of bits. It is typically eight bits, but there are those who use non-standard byte sizes. Bytes are usually measured in large groups, and the term "kilobyte" (often abbreviated as K) means one-thousand twenty-four (1024) bytes; the term "megabyte" (often abbreviated as M) means one-thousand twenty-four (1024) K; the term gigabyte (often abbreviated as G) means one-thousand twenty-four (1024) M; and the term "terabyte" (often abbreviated as T) means one-thousand twenty-four (1024) G. Memory is typically measured in kilobytes or megabytes, and disk space is typically measured in megabytes or gigabytes. Note that the multipliers here are 1024 instead of the more common 1000 as would be used in the metric system. This is to make it easier to work with the binary number system.

bytecode
Sometimes computer languages that are said to be either interpreted or compiled are in fact neither and are more accurately said to be somewhere in between. Such languages are compiled into bytecode which is then interpreted on the target system. Bytecode tends to be binary but will work on any machine with the appropriate runtime environment (or virtual machine) for it.

C
C is one of the most popular computer languages in the world, and quite possibly *the* most popular. It is a compiled language widely supported on many platforms. It tends to be more portable than FORTRAN but less portable than Java; it has been standardized by ANSI as "ANSI C" -- older versions are called either "K&R C" or "Kernighan and Ritchie C" (in honor of C's creators), or sometimes just "classic C". Fast and simple, it can be applied to all manner of general purpose tasks. C compilers are made by several companies, but the free GNU version (gcc) is still considered one of the best. Newer C-like object-oriented languages include both Java and C++.

C#
C# is a compiled object-oriented language based heavily on C++ with some Java features.

C++
C++ is a compiled object-oriented language. Based heavily on C, C++ is nearly as fast and can often be thought of as being just C with added features. It is currently probably the second most popular object-oriented language, but it has the drawback of being fairly complex -- the much simpler but somewhat slower Java is probably the most popular object-oriented language. Note that C++ was developed independently of the somewhat similar Objective-C; it is however related to Objective-C++.

C64/128
The Commodore 64 computer was a massively successful model of computer with estimated

tens of millions units sold. Its big brother, the Commodore 128, was not quite as popular but still sold several million units. Both units sported ROM-based BASIC and used it as a default "OS". The C128 also came with CP/M (it was a not-often-exercised option on the C64). In their later days they were also packaged with GEOS. Both are based on 65xx family processors.

chain
Some computer devices support chaining, the ability to string multiple devices in a sequence plugged into just one computer port. Often, but not always, such a chain will require some sort of terminator to mark the end. For an example, a SCSI scanner may be plugged into a SCSI CD-ROM drive that is plugged into a SCSI hard drive that is in turn plugged into the main computer. For all these components to work properly, the scanner would also have to have a proper terminator in use. Device chaining has been around a long time, and it is interesting to note that C64/128 serial devices supported it from the very beginning.

character set
Since in reality all a computer can store are series of zeros and ones, representing common things like text takes a little work. The solution is to view the series of zeros and ones instead as a sequence of bytes, and map each one to a particular letter, number, or symbol. The full mapping is called a character set. The most popular character set is commonly referred to as ASCII. The second most popular character set is Unicode

COBOL
The Common Business Oriented Language is a language developed back in 1959. While it was relatively portable, it was disliked by many professional programmers simply because COBOL programs tended to be physically longer than equivalent programs written in almost any other language in common use.

compiled
If a program is compiled, its original human-readable source has been converted into a form more easily used by a computer prior to it being run. Such programs will generally run more quickly than interpreted programs, because time was pre-spent in the compilation phase. A program that compiles other programs is called a compiler.

compression
It is often possible to remove redundant information or capitalize on patterns in data to make a file smaller. Usually when a file has been compressed, it cannot be used until it is uncompressed. Image files are common exceptions, though, as many popular image file formats have compression built-in.

cookie
A cookie is a small file that a web page on another machine writes to your personal machine's disk to store various bits of information. Many people strongly detest cookies and the whole idea of them, and most browsers allow the reception of cookies to be disabled or at least selectively disabled. Sites that maintain shopping carts or remember a reader's last position have legitimate uses for cookies. Sites without such functionality that still spew cookies with distant (or worse, non-existent) expiration dates should perhaps be treated with a little caution.

crash
If a bug in a program is severe enough, it can cause that program to crash, or to become inoperable without being restarted. On machines that are not multitasking, the entire machine will crash and have to be rebooted. On machines that are only partially multitasking the entire machine will sometimes crash and have to be rebooted. On machines that are fully multitasking, the machine should never crash and require a reboot.

crippleware
Crippleware is a variant of shareware that will either self-destruct after its trial period or has built-in limitations to its functionality that get removed after its purchase.

CSS
Cascading style sheets are used in conjunction with HTML and XHTML to define the layout of web pages. While CSS is how current web pages declare how they should be displayed, it

tends not to be supported well (if at all) by ancient browsers.
desktop publisher
A program for creating newspapers, magazines, books, etc. Some common desktop publishing programs include Adobe InDesign, Canva, Affinity Publisher and Microsoft Publisher.
DHTML
Dynamic HTML is simply the combined use of both CSS and JavaScript together in the same document; a more extreme form is called AJaX. Note that DHTML is quite different from the similarly named DTML.
dict
A protocol used for looking up definitions across a network (in particular the Internet).
digital camera
A digital camera looks and behaves like a regular camera, except instead of using film, it stores the image it sees in memory as a file for later transfer to a computer. Many digital cameras offer additional storage besides their own internal memory; a few sport some sort of disk but the majority utilize some sort of flash card. Digital cameras were eventually integrated into mobile phones and are now a dominant element of smartphone technology.
DNS
Domain name service is the means by which a name (like www.saugus.net or ftp.saugus.net) gets converted into a real Internet address that points to a particular machine.
DoS
In a denial of service attack, many individual (usually compromised) computers are used to try and simultaneously access the same public resource with the intent of overburdening it so that it will not be able to adequately serve its normal users.
DOS
A disk operating system manages disks and other system resources. Sort of a subset of OSes, sort of an archaic term for the same. MS-DOS is the most popular program currently calling itself a DOS. CP/M was the most popular prior to MS-DOS.
download
To download a file is to copy it from a remote computer to your own. The opposite is upload.
driver
A driver is a piece of software that works with the OS to control a particular piece of hardware, like a printer, scanner or mouse.
DRM
DRM can stand for either Digital Rights Management or Digital Restrictions Management. In either case, DRM is used to place restrictions upon the usage of digital media ranging from software to music to video.
DTML
The Document Template Mark-up Language is a subset of SGML and a superset of HTML used for creating documents that dynamically adapt to external conditions using its own custom tags and a little bit of Python. Note that it is quite different from the similarly named DHTML.
EDBIC
The EDBIC character set is similar to (but less popular than) the ASCII character set in concept, but is significantly different in layout. It tends to be found only on old machines.
embedded
An embedded system is a computer that lives inside another device and acts as a component of that device. For example, cars have an embedded computer under the hood that helps regulate much of their day-to-day operation. An embedded file lives inside another and acts as a portion of that file. This is frequently seen with HTML files having embedded audio files; audio files often embedded in HTML include AU files, MIDI files, SID files, WAV files, AIFF files, and MOD files. Most browsers will ignore these files unless an appropriate plug-in is present.

emulator

An emulator is a program that allows one computer platform to mimic another for the purposes of running its software. Typically (but not always) running a program through an emulator will not be quite as pleasant an experience as running it on the real system.

environment

An environment (sometimes also called a runtime environment) is a collection of external variable items or parameters that a program can access when run. Information about the computer's hardware and the user can often be found in the environment.

extension

Filename extensions allow a grouping of different file types by putting a tag at the end of the name, such as .doc or .pdf.

FAQ

A frequently asked questions file attempts to provide answers for all commonly asked questions related to a given topic.

FireWire

An incredibly fast type of serial port that offers many of the best features of SCSI at a lower price. Faster than most types of parallel port, a single FireWire port is capable of chaining many devices without the need of a terminator. FireWire is similar in many respects to USB but is significantly faster and somewhat more expensive. It is heavily used for connecting audio/video devices to computers, but is also used for connecting storage devices like drives and other assorted devices like printers and scanners.

fixed width

As applied to a font, fixed width means that every character takes up the same amount of space. That is, an "i" will be just as wide as an "m" with empty space being used for padding. The opposite is variable width. The most common fixed width font is Courier.

flash

Flash memory is similar to RAM. It has one significant advantage: it does not lose its contents when power is lost; it has two main disadvantages: it is slower, and it eventually wears out. Flash memory is frequently found in PCMCIA cards.

font

In a simplistic sense, a font can be thought of as the physical description of a character set. While the character set will define what sets of bits map to what letters, numbers, and other symbols, the font will define what each letter, number, and other symbol looks like. Fonts can be either fixed width or variable width and independently, either bitmapped or vectored. The size of the large characters in a font is typically measured in points.

FORTRAN

FORTRAN stands for formula translation and is the oldest computer language in the world. Today languages like C and Java are more popular, but FORTRAN is still heavily used in military software. It is somewhat amusing to note that when FORTRAN was first released back in 1958 its advocates thought that it would mean the end of software bugs. In truth of course by making the creation of more complex software practical, computer languages have merely created new types of software bugs.

FreeBSD

A free variant of Berkeley UNIX available for Alpha and x86 based machines. It was not as popular as Linux.

freeware

Freeware is software that is available for free with no strings attached. The quality is often superb as the authors are also generally users.

FTP

The file transfer protocol is one of the most commonly used methods of copying files across the Internet. It has its origins on UNIX machines, but has been adapted to almost every type of computer in existence and is built into many browsers. Most FTP programs have two modes of operation, ASCII, and binary. Transmitting an ASCII file via the ASCII mode of operation is more efficient and cleaner. Transmitting a binary file via the ASCII mode of operation will result in a broken binary file. Thus the FTP programs that do not support both modes of operation will typically only do the binary mode, as binary transfers are capable of transferring both kinds of data without corruption.

gateway

A gateway connects otherwise separate computer networks.

GHz & gigahertz

One gigahertz is equivalent to 1000 megahertz, or 1,000,000,000 hertz.

GNOME

The GNU network object model environment was a popular free window manager (and much more -- as its name touts, it is more of a desktop environment) that ran under X-Windows. It was a part of the GNU project.

GNU

GNU stands for GNU's not UNIX and is thus a recursive acronym (and unlike the animal name, the "G" here is pronounced). At any rate, the GNU project is an effort by the Free Software Foundation (FSF) to make all of the traditional UNIX utilities free for whoever wants them.

HP-UX

HP-UX is the version of UNIX designed by Hewlett-Packard to work with their PA-RISC and 68xx based machines.

HTML

The Hypertext Mark-up Language is the language currently most frequently used to express web pages. Every browser has the built-in ability to understand HTML. Some browsers can additionally understand Java and browse FTP areas. HTML is a proper subset of SGML.

http

The hypertext transfer protocol is the native protocol of browsers and is most typically used to transfer HTML formatted files. The secure version is called "https".

Hz & hertz

Hertz means cycles per second, and makes no assumptions about what is cycling. So, for example, if a fluorescent light flickers once per jiffy, it has a 60 Hz flicker. More typical for computers would be a program that runs once per jiffy and thus has a 60 Hz frequency, or larger units of hertz like kHz, MHz, GHz, or THz.

iCalendar

The iCalendar standard refers to the format used to store calendar type information (including events, to-do items, and journal entries) on the Internet. iCalendar data can be found on some World-Wide-Web pages or attached to e-mail messages.

icon

A small graphical display representing an object, action, or modifier of some sort.

Inform

A compiled, object-oriented language optimized for creating interactive fiction.

infrared communications

A device with an infrared port can communicate with other devices at a distance by beaming infrared light signals. Two incompatible protocols are used for infrared communications: IrDA and ASK. Many devices support both.

Instant Messenger

AOL's Instant Messenger was a means of chatting over the Internet in real-time. It allowed both open group discussions and private conversations. Instant Messenger used a different, proprietary protocol from the more standard IRC, and was not supported on as many platforms.

interactive fiction
Interactive fiction (often abbreviated "IF" or "I-F") is a form of literature unique to the computer. While the reader cannot influence the direction of a typical story, the reader plays a more active role in an interactive fiction story and completely controls its direction. Interactive fiction works come in all the sizes and genres available to standard fiction, and in fact are not always even fiction per se (interactive tutorials exist and are slowly becoming more common).

interpreted
If a program is interpreted, its actual human-readable source is read as it is run by the computer. This is generally a slower process than if the program being run has already been compiled.

Intranet
An intranet is a private network. There are many intranets scattered all over the world. Some are connected to the Internet via gateways.

IP
IP is the family of protocols that makes up the Internet.

IRC
Internet relay chat is a means of chatting over the Internet in real-time. It allows both open group discussions and private conversations.

IrDA
The Infrared Data Association (IrDA) is a voluntary organization of various manufacturers working together to ensure that the infrared communications between different computers, printers, digital cameras, remote controls, etc. are all compatible with each other regardless of brand. The term is also often used to designate an IrDA compliant infrared communications port on a device. Informally, a device able to communicate via IrDA compliant infrared is sometimes simply said to "have IrDA". There is also an earlier, incompatible, and usually slower type of infrared communications still in use called ASK.

IRI
An Internationalized Resource Identifier is just a URI with i18n.

IRIX
The variant of UNIX designed by Silicon Graphics, Inc. IRIX machines are known for their graphics capabilities and were initially optimized for multimedia applications.

ISDN
An integrated service digital network line can be simply looked at as a digital phone line. ISDN connections to the Internet can be four times faster than the fastest regular phone connection, and because it is a digital connection a modem is not needed. Any computer hooked up to ISDN will typically require other special equipment in lieu of the modem, however. Also, both phone companies and ISPs charge more for ISDN connections than regular modem connections.

ISP
An Internet service provider is a company that provides Internet support for other entities.

Java
A computer language designed to be both fairly lightweight and extremely portable. It is tightly bound to the web as it is the primary language for web applets. There has also been an OS based on Java for use on small hand-held, embedded, and network computers. It is called JavaOS. Java can be either interpreted or compiled. For web applet use it is almost always interpreted. While its interpreted form tends not to be very fast, its compiled form can often rival languages like C++ for speed. It is important to note however that speed is not Java's primary purpose -- raw speed is considered secondary to portabilty and ease of use.

JavaScript
JavaScript (in spite of its name) has nothing whatsoever to do with Java (in fact, it's arguably more like Newton Script than Java). JavaScript is an interpreted language built into a browser to

provide a relatively simple means of adding interactivity to web pages. It is only supported on a few different browsers, and tends not to work exactly the same on different versions. Thus its use on the Internet is somewhat restricted to fairly simple programs. On intranets where there are usually fewer browser versions in use, JavaScript has been used to implement much more complex and impressive programs.

jiffy
A jiffy is 1/60 of a second. Jiffies are to seconds as seconds are to minutes.

joystick
A joystick is a physical device typically used to control objects on a computer screen. It is frequently used for games and sometimes used in place of a mouse. Today, joysticks are used for gaming, robotics, medical research, virtual reality (VR), and industrial control systems.

JSON
The JSON is used for data interchange between programs, an area in which the ubiquitous XML is not too well-suited. JSON is lightweight and works extremely cleanly with languages including JavaScript, Python, Java, C++, and many others.

JSON-RPC
JSON-RPC is like XML-RPC but is significantly more lightweight since it uses JSON in lieu of XML.

kernel
The very heart of an OS is often called its kernel. It will usually (at minimum) provide some libraries that give programmers access to its various features.

kHz & kilohertz
One kilohertz is equivalent to 1000 hertz. Some older computers have clock speeds measured in kHz.

LDAP
The Lightweight Directory Access Protocol provides a means of sharing address book type of information across an intranet or even across the Internet. Note too that "address book type of information" here is pretty broad; it often includes not just human addresses, but machine addresses, printer configurations, and similar.

library
A selection of routines used by programmers to make computers do particular things.

lightweight
Something that is lightweight will not consume computer resources (such as RAM and disk space) too much and will thus run on less expensive computer systems.

Linux
One of the fastest, most robust, and powerful multitasking OS systems. Linux can be downloaded for free or be purchased for a small service charge. Linux is available for more hardware combinations than any other OS. Fast, reliable, stable, and inexpensive, Linux is popular with ISPs, software developers, and home hobbyists alike.

load
There are two popular meanings for load. The first means to fetch some data or a program from a disk and store it in memory. The second indicates the amount of work a component (especially a processor) is being made to do.

Logo
Logo is an interpreted language designed by Papert in 1966 to be a tool for helping people (especially kids) learn computer programming concepts. In addition to being used for that purpose, it is often used as a language for controlling mechanical robots and other similar devices. Logo interfaces even exist for building block / toy robot sets. Logo uses a special graphics cursor called "the turtle", and Logo is itself sometimes called "Turtle Graphics". Logo is quite portable but not particularly fast. Versions can be found on almost every computer platform in the world. Additionally, some other languages (notably some Pascal versions) provide Logo-

like interfaces for graphics-intensive programming.

lossy

If a process is lossy, it means that a little quality is lost when it is performed. If a format is lossy, it means that putting data into that format (or possibly even manipulating it in that format) will cause some slight loss. Lossy processes and formats are typically used for performance or resource utilization reasons. The opposite of lossy is lossless.

Lua

Lua is a simple interpreted language. It is extremely portable, and free versions exist for most platforms.

Mac OS

Mac OS is the OS used on Macintosh computers. There are two distinctively different versions of it; everything prior to version 10 (sometimes called Mac OS Classic) and everything version 10 or later (called Mac OS X).

Mac OS Classic

The OS created by Apple and originally used by Macs is frequently (albeit slightly incorrectly) referred to as Mac OS Classic (officially Mac OS Classic is this original OS running under the modern Mac OS X in emulation. Mac OS combines the functionality of both an OS and a window manager and is often considered to be the easiest OS to use. It is partially multitasking but will still sometimes crash when dealing with a buggy program. It is probably the second most popular OS, next only to Windows 'XP (although it is quickly losing ground to Mac OS X) and has excellent driver support and boasts a fair selection of games. Mac OS will run on PowerPC and 68xx based machines.

Mac OS X

Mac OS X (originally called Rhapsody) is the industrial strength OS produced by Apple to run on both PowerPC and x86 systems (replacing what is often referred to as Mac OS Classic. Mac OS X is at its heart a variant of UNIX and possesses its underlying power (and the ability to run many of the traditional UNIX tools, including the GNU tools).

machine language

Machine language consists of the raw numbers that can be directly understood by a particular processor. Each processor's machine language will be different from other processors' machine language. Although called "machine language", it is not usually what people think of when talking about computer languages. Machine language dressed up with mnemonics to make it a bit more human-readable is called assembly language.

Macintosh

A Macintosh (or a Mac for short) is a computer system that has Mac OS for its OS. There are a few different companies that have produced Macs, but by far the largest is Apple. The oldest Macs are based on the 68xx processor; somewhat more recent Macs on the PowerPC processor, and current Macs on the x86 processor. The Macintosh was really the first general purpose computer to employ a GUI.

MacTel

An x86 based system running some flavor of Mac OS.

mainframe

A mainframe is any computer larger than a small piece of furniture. A modern mainframe is more powerful than a modern workstation, but more expensive and more difficult to maintain.

MathML

The Math Mark-up Language is a subset of XML used to represent mathematical formulae and equations. Typically it is found embedded within XHTML documents, although as of this writing not all popular browsers support it.

megahertz

A million cycles per second, abbreviated MHz. This is often used misleadingly to indicate processor speed, because while one might expect that a higher number would indicate a faster processor, that logic only holds true within a given type of processors as different types of processors are capable of doing different amounts of work within a cycle. For a current example, either a 200 MHz PowerPC or a 270 MHz SPARC will outperform a 300 MHz Pentium.

middleware
Software designed to sit in between an OS and applications. Common examples are Java and Tcl/Tk.

MIME
The multi-purpose Internet mail extensions specification describes a means of sending non-ASCII data (such as images, sounds, foreign symbols, etc.) through e-mail. It commonly utilizes bcode.

MMX
Multimedia extensions were built into some x86 CPUs to provide better performance for certain operations, most notably graphics and sound. It is similar to AltiVec on the PowerPC CPUs. Like AltiVec, it requires special software for full performance benefits to be realized.

MOB
A movable object is a graphical object that is manipulated separately from the background. These are seen all the time in computer games. When implemented in hardware, MOBs are sometimes called sprites.

Modula-2 & Modula-3
Modula-2 is a procedural language based on Pascal by its original author in around the 1977 1979 time period. Modula-3 is an intended successor that adds support for object-oriented constructs (among other things). Modula-2 can be either compiled or interpreted, while Modula-3 tends to be just a compiled language.

MOTD
A message **of** the day. Many computers (particularly more capable ones) are configured to display a MOTD when accessed remotely.

MS-DOS
The DOS produced by Microsoft. Early versions of it bear striking similarities to the earlier CP/M, but it utilizes simpler commands. It provides only a CLI, but either OS/2, Windows 3.1, Windows '95, Windows '98, Windows ME, or GEOS may be run on top of it to provide a GUI. It only runs on x86 based machines.

MS-Windows
MS-Windows is the name collectively given to several somewhat incompatible OSes all produced by Microsoft. The latest Windows update is Windows 11, version 23H2.

MUD
A multi-user dimension (also sometimes called multi-user dungeon, but in either case abbreviated to "MUD") is sort of a combination between the online chatting abilities provided by something like IRC and a role-playing game. A MUD built with object oriented principles in mind is called a "Multi-user dimension object-oriented", or MOO. Yet another variant is called a "multi-user shell", or MUSH. Still other variants are called multi-user role-playing environments (MURPE) and multi-user environments (MUSE). There are probably more. In all cases the differences will be mostly academic to the regular user, as the same software is used to connect to all of them. Software to connect to MUDs can be found for most platforms, and there are even Java based ones that can run from within a browser.

multitasking
Some OSes have built into them the ability to do several things at once. This is called multitasking, and has been in use since the late sixties / early seventies. Since this ability is built into the software, the overall system will be slower running two things at once than it will be running just one thing. A system may have more than one processor built into it though, and such a system will be capable of running multiple things at once with less of a performance hit.

nagware
Nagware is a variant of shareware that will frequently remind its users to register.

NetBSD
A free variant of Berkeley UNIX available for Alpha, x86, 68xx, PA-RISC, SPARC, PowerPC, ARM, and many other types of machines. Its emphasis is on portability.
newbie
A newbie is a novice to the online world or computers in general.
news
Usenet news can generally be thought of as public e-mail as that is generally the way it behaves. In reality, it is implemented by different software and is often accessed by different programs. Different newsgroups adhere to different topics, and some are "moderated", meaning that humans will try to manually remove off-topic posts, especially spam. Most established newsgroups have a FAQ, and people are strongly encouraged to read the FAQ prior to posting.
Newton
Although Newton is officially the name of the lightweight OS developed by Apple to run on its MessagePad line of PDAs, it is often used to mean the MessagePads (and compatible PDAs) themselves and thus the term "Newton OS" is often used for clarity. The Newton OS is remarkably powerful; it is fully multitasking in spite of the fact that it was designed for small machines. It is optimized for hand-held use, but will readily transfer data to all manner of desktop machines. Historically it was the first PDA. Recently Apple announced that it will discontinue further development of the Newton platform, but will instead work to base future hand-held devices on either Mac OS or Mac OS X with some effort dedicated to making the new devices capable of running current Newton programs.
Newton book
Newton books provide all the functionality of ordinary books but add searching and hypertext capabilities. The format was invented for the Newton to provide a means of making volumes of data portable, and is particularly popular in the medical community as most medical references are available as Newton books and carrying around a one pound Newton is preferable to carrying around twenty pounds of books, especially when it comes to looking up something. In addition to medical books, numerous references, most of the classics, and many contemporary works of fiction are available as Newton books. Most fiction is available for free, most references cost money. Newton books are somewhat more capable than the similar Palm DOC; both are specific types of e-books.
nybble
A nybble is half a byte, or four bits. It is a case of computer whimsy; it only stands to reason that a small byte should be called a nybble. Some authors spell it with an "i" instead of the "y", but the "y" is the original form.
object-oriented
The term "object-oriented" applies to a philosophy of software creation. Often this philosophy is referred to as object-oriented design (sometimes abbreviated as OOD), and programs written with it in mind are referred to as object-oriented programs (often abbreviated OOP). Programming languages designed to help facilitate it are called object-oriented languages (sometimes abbreviated as 00L) and databases built with it in mind are called object-oriented databases (sometimes abbreviated as OODB or less fortunately OOD). The general notion is that an object-oriented approach to creating software starts with modeling the real-world problems trying to be solved in familiar real-world ways, and carries the analogy all the way down to structure of the program. This is of course a great over-simplification. Numerous object-oriented programming languages exist including: Java, C++, Modula-2, Newton Script, and ADA.
Objective-C & ObjC
Objective-C (often called "ObjC" for short) is a compiled object-oriented language. Based heavily on C, Objective-C is nearly as fast and can often be thought of as being just C with added features. Note that it was developed independently of C++; its object-oriented extensions are more in the style of Smalltalk. It is however related to Objective-C++.
Objective-C++ & ObjC++

Objective-C++ (often called "ObjC++" for short) is a curious hybrid of Objective-C and C++, allowing the syntax of both to coexist in the same source files.

office suite
An office suite is a collection of programs including at minimum a word processor, spreadsheet, drawing program, and minimal database program. Some popular office suites include Google Workspace, Microsoft 365, iWork, LibreOffice, Polaris Office and OpenOffice.

open source
Open source software goes one step beyond freeware. Not only does it provide the software for free, it provides the original source code used to create the software. Thus, curious users can poke around with it to see how it works, and advanced users can modify it to make it work better for them. By its nature, open source software is pretty well immune to all types of computer virus.

OpenBSD
A free variant of Berkeley UNIX available for Alpha, x86, 68xx, PA-RISC, SPARC, and PowerPC based machines. Its emphasis is on security.

OpenDocument & ODF
OpenDocument (or ODF for short) is the suite of open, XML-based office suite application formats defined by the OASIS consortium. It defines a platform-neutral, non-proprietary way of storing documents.

OpenGL
A low-level 3D graphics library with an emphasis on speed developed by SGI.

OS/2
OS/2 is the OS designed by IBM to run on x86 based machines. It is semi-compatible with MS-Windows. IBM's more industrial strength OS is called AIX.

Palm Pilot
The Palm Pilot (also called both just Palm and just Pilot, officially now just Palm) was the most popular PDA in use. It was one of the least capable PDAs but also one of the smallest and least expensive. While not as full-featured as many of the other PDAs (such as the Newton), it performed what features it did have quite well.

parallel
Loosely speaking, parallel implies a situation where multiple things can be done simultaneously, like having multiple check-out lines each serving people all at once. Parallel connections are by their nature more expensive than serial ones, but usually faster. Also, in a related use of the word, often multitasking computers are said to be capable of running multiple programs in parallel.

partition
Sometimes due to hardware limitations, disks have to be divided into smaller pieces. These pieces are called partitions.

Pascal
Named after the mathematician Blaise Pascal, Pascal is a language designed by Niklaus Wirth originally in 1968 (and heavily revised in 1972) mostly for purposes of education and training people how to write computer programs. It is a typically compiled language but is still usually slower than C or FORTRAN. Wirth also created a more powerful object-oriented Pascal-like language called Modula-2.

PC-DOS
The DOS produced by IBM designed to work like MS-DOS. Early versions of it bear striking similarities to the earlier CP/M, but it utilizes simpler commands. It provides only a CLI, but either Windows 3.1 or GEOS may be run on top of it to provide a GUI. It only runs on x86 based machines.

PCMCIA
The Personal Computer Memory Card International Association is a standards body that concern themselves with PC Card technology. Often the PC Cards themselves are referred

to as "PCMCIA cards". Frequently flash memory can be found in PC card form.
Perl
Perl is an interpreted language extremely popular for web applications.
PET
The Commodore PET (Personal Electronic Transactor) is an early (circa 1977-1980, around the same time as the Apple][) home computer featuring a ROM-based BASIC developed by Microsoft which it uses as a default "OS". It is based on the 65xx family of processors and is the precursor to the VIC-20.
PHP
Named with a recursive acronym (PHP: Hypertext Preprocessor), PHP provides a means of creating web pages that dynamically modify themselves on the fly.
ping
Ping is a protocol designed to check across a network to see if a particular computer is "alive" or not. Computers that recognize the ping will report back their status. Computers that are down will not report back anything at all.
pixel
The smallest distinct point on a computer display is called a pixel.
plug-in
A plug-in is a piece of software designed not to run on its own but rather work in cooperation with a separate application to increase that application's abilities.
point
There are two common meanings for this word. The first is in the geometric sense; a position in space without size. Of course as applied to computers it must take up some space in practice (even if not in theory) and it is thus sometimes synonymous with pixel. The other meaning is related most typically to fonts and regards size. The exact meaning of it in this sense will unfortunately vary somewhat from person to person, but will often mean 1/72 of an inch. Even when it does not exactly mean 1/72 of an inch, larger point sizes always indicate larger fonts.
PowerPC
The PowerPC is a RISC processor developed in a collaborative effort between IBM, Apple, and Motorola. It is currently produced by a few different companies, of course including its original developers. A few different OSes run on PowerPC based machines, including Mac OS, AIX, Solaris, Windows NT, Linux, Mac OS X, BeOS, and AmigaOS. At any given time, the fastest processor in the world is usually either a PowerPC or an Alpha, but sometimes SPARCs and PA-RISCs make the list, too.
proprietary
This simply means to be supplied by only one vendor. It is commonly misused. Currently, most processors are non-proprietary, some systems are non-proprietary, and every OS (except for arguably Linux) is proprietary.
protocol
A protocol is a means of communication used between computers. As long as both computers recognize the same protocol, they can communicate without too much difficulty over the same network or even via a simple direct modem connection regardless whether or not they are themselves of the same type. This means that WinTel boxes, Macs, Amigas, UNIX machines, etc., can all talk with one another provided they agree on a common protocol first.
queue
A queue is a waiting list of things to be processed. Many computers provide printing queues, for example. If something is being printed and the user requests that another item be printed, the second item will sit in the printer queue until the first item finishes printing at which point it will be removed from the queue and get printed itself.
RAM
Random access memory is the short-term memory of a computer. Any information stored in

RAM will be lost if power goes out, but the computer can read from RAM far more quickly than from a drive.

random access
Also called "dynamic access" this indicates that data can be selected without having to skip over earlier data first. This is the way that a CD, record, laserdisc, or DVD will behave -- it is easy to selectively play a particular track without having to fast forward through earlier tracks. The other common behavior is called sequential access.

RDF
The Resource Description Framework is built upon an XML base and provides a more modern means of accessing data from Internet resources. It can provide metadata (including annotations) for web pages making (among other things) searching more capable. It is also being used to refashion some existing formats like RSS and iCalendar; in the former case it is already in place (at least for newer RSS versions), but it is still experimental in the latter case.

real-time
Something that happens in real-time will keep up with the events around it and never give any sort of "please wait" message.

Rexx
The Restructured Extended Executor is an interpreted language designed primarily to be embedded in other applications in order to make them consistently programmable, but also to be easy to learn and understand.

RISC
Reduced instruction set computing is one of the two main types of processor design in use today, the other being CISC. The fastest processors in the world today are all RISC designs. There are several popular RISC processors, including Alphas, ARMs, PA-RISCs, PowerPCs, and SPARCs.

robot
A robot (or 'bot for short) in the computer sense is a program designed to automate some task, often just sending messages or collecting information. A spider is a type of robot designed to traverse the web performing some task (usually collecting data).

robust
The adjective robust is used to describe programs that are better designed, have fewer bugs, and are less likely to crash.

ROM
Read-only memory is similar to RAM only cannot be altered and does not lose its contents when power is removed.

RSS
RSS stands for either Rich Site Summary, Really Simple Syndication, or **RDF** Site Summary, depending upon whom you ask. The general idea is that it can provide brief summaries of articles that appear in full on a web site. It is well-formed XML, and newer versions are even more specifically well-formed RDF.

Ruby
Ruby is an interpreted, object-oriented language. Ruby was fairly heavily influenced by Perl, so people familiar with that language can typically transition to Ruby easily.

scanner
A scanner is a piece of hardware that will examine a picture and produce a computer file that represents what it sees. A digital camera is a related device. Each has its own limitations.

script
A script is a series of OS commands. The term "batch file" means much the same thing, but is a bit dated. Typically the same sort of situations in which one would say DOS instead of OS, it would also be appropriate to say batch file instead of script. Scripts can be run like programs, but tend to perform simpler tasks. When a script is run, it is always interpreted.

SCSI
Loosely speaking, a disk format sometimes used by MS-Windows, Mac OS, AmigaOS, and (almost always) UNIX. Generally SCSI is superior (but more expensive) to IDE, but it varies somewhat with system load and the individual SCSI and IDE components themselves. The quick rundown is that: SCSI-I and SCSI-II will almost always outperform IDE; EIDE will almost always outperform SCSI-I and SCSI-II; SCSI-III and UltraSCSI will almost always outperform EIDE; and heavy system loads give an advantage to SCSI. Note that although loosely speaking it is just a format difference, it is deep down a hardware difference.

sequential access
This indicates that data cannot be selected without having to skip over earlier data first. This is the way that a cassette or video tape will behave. The other common behavior is called random access.

serial
Loosely speaking, serial implies something that has to be done linearly, one at a time, like people being served in a single check-out line. Serial connections are by their nature less expensive than parallel connections (including things like SCSI) but are typically slower.

server
A server is a computer designed to provide various services for an entire network. It is typically either a workstation or a mainframe because it will usually be expected to handle far greater loads than ordinary desktop systems. The load placed on servers also necessitates that they utilize robust OSes, as a crash on a system that is currently being used by many people is far worse than a crash on a system that is only being used by one person.

SGML
The Standard Generalized Mark-up Language provides an extremely generalized level of mark-up. More common mark-up languages like HTML and XML are actually just popular subsets of SGML.

shareware
Shareware is software made for profit that allows a trial period before purchase. Typically shareware can be freely downloaded, used for a period of weeks (or sometimes even months), and either purchased or discarded after it has been learned whether or not it will satisfy the user's needs.

shell
A CLI designed to simplify complex OS commands. Some OSes (like AmigaOS, the Hurd, and UNIX) have built-in support to make the concurrent use of multiple shells easy. Common shells include the Korn Shell (ksh), the Bourne Shell (sh or bsh), the Bourne-Again Shell, (bash or bsh), the C-Shell (csh), etc.

SIMM
A physical component used to add RAM to a computer. Similar to, but incompatible with, DIMMs.

Smalltalk
Smalltalk is an efficient language for writing computer programs. Historically it is one of the first object-oriented languages, and is not only used today in its pure form but shows its influence in other languages like Objective-C.

spam
Generally spam is unwanted, unrequested e-mail or some other form of contact. It is typically sent out in bulk to huge address lists that were automatically generated by various robots endlessly searching the Internet and newsgroups for things that resemble e-mail addresses.

SPARC
The SPARC was a RISC processor developed by Sun.

sprite
The term sprite originally referred to a small MOB, usually implemented in hardware. Lately it

is also being used to refer to a single image used piecemeal within a Web site in order to avoid incurring the time penalty of downloading multiple files.

SQL

SQL (pronounced Sequel) is an interpreted language specially designed for database access. It is supported by virtually every major modern database system.

SVG

Scalable Vector Graphics data is an XML file that is used to hold graphical data that can be resized without loss of quality. SVG data can be kept in its own file, or even embedded within a web page (although not all browsers are capable of displaying such data).

Tonic

The Tool Command Language is a portable interpreted computer language designed to be easy to use. Tk is a GUI toolkit for Tcl. Tcl is a fairly popular language for both integrating existing applications and for creating Web applets (note that applets written in Tcl are often called Tcklets). Tcl/Tk is available for free for most platforms, and plug-ins are available to enable many browsers to play Tcklets.

TCP/IP

TCP/IP is a protocol for computer networks. The Internet is largely built on top of TCP/IP (it is the more reliable of the two primary Internet Protocols -- TCP stands for Transmission Control Protocol).

terminator

A terminator is a dedicated device used to mark the end of a device chain (as is most typically found with SCSI devices). If such a chain is not properly terminated, weird results can occur.

TEX

TEX (pronounced "tek") is a freely available, industrial strength typesetting program that can be run on many different platforms. These qualities make it exceptionally popular in schools, and frequently software developed at a university will have its documentation in TEX format. TEX is not limited to educational use, though; many professional books were typeset with TEX. TEX's primary drawback is that it can be quite difficult to set up initially.

THz & terahertz

One terahertz is equivalent to 1000 gigahertz.

TrackBack

TrackBacks essentially provide a means whereby different web sites can post messages to one another not just to inform each other about citations, but also to alert one another of related resources. Typically, a blog may display quotations from another blog through the use of TrackBacks.

UDP/IP

UDP/IP is a protocol for computer networks. It is the faster of the two primary Internet Protocols. UDP stands for User Datagram Protocol.

Unicode

The Unicode character set is a superset of the ASCII character set with provisions made for handling international symbols and characters from other languages. Unicode is sixteen bit, so takes up roughly twice the space as simple ASCII, but is correspondingly more flexible.

UNIX

UNIX is a family of OSes, each being made by a different company or organization but all offering a very similar look and feel. It cannot quite be considered non-proprietary, however, as the differences between different vendor's versions can be significant (it is still generally possible to switch from one vendor's UNIX to another without too much effort; today the differences between different UNIXes are similar to the differences between the different MS-Windows; historically there were two different UNIX camps, Berkeley / BSD and AT&T / System V, but the assorted vendors have worked together to minimize the differences). The free variant Linux is one of the closest things to a current, non-proprietary OS; its development is controlled by a non-profit organization and its distribution is provided by several companies. UNIX is powerful; it is fully multitasking and can do pretty much anything that any OS can do (look to the Hurd if you need a more powerful OS). With power comes complexity, however, and UNIX tends not to be overly friendly to beginners (although those who think UNIX is difficult or cryptic apparently have not used CP/M). Window managers are available for UNIX (running under X-Windows) and once properly configured common operations will be almost as simple on a UNIX machine as on a Mac. Out of all the OSes in current use, UNIX has the greatest range of hardware support. It will run on machines built around many different processors.

upload

To upload a file is to copy it from your computer to a remote computer. The opposite is download.

UPS

An uninterrupted power supply uses heavy duty batteries to help smooth out its input power source.

URI

A Uniform Resource Identifier is basically just a unique address for almost any type of resource. It is similar to but more general than a URL; in fact, it may also be a URN.

URL

A Uniform Resource Locator is basically just an address for a file that can be given to a browser. It starts with a protocol type (such as http, ftp, or gopher) and is followed by a colon, machine name, and file name in UNIX style. Optionally an octothorpe character "#" and and arguments will follow the file name; this can be used to further define position within a page and perform a few other tricks. Similar to but less general than a URI.

URN

A Uniform Resource Name is basically just a unique address for almost any type of resource unlike a URL it will probably not resolve with a browser.

USB

A really fast type of serial port that offers many of the best features of SCSI without the price. Faster than many types of parallel port, a single USB port is capable of chaining many devices without the need of a terminator. USB is much slower (but somewhat less expensive) than FireWire.

uucode

The point of uucode is to allow 8-bit binary data to be transferred through the more common 7-bit ASCII channels (most especially e-mail). The facilities for dealing with uucoded files exist for many different machine types, and the most common programs are called "uuencode" for encoding the original binary file into a 7-bit file and "uudecode" for restoring the original binary file from the encoded one. Sometimes different uuencode and uudecode programs will work in subtly different manners causing annoying compatibility problems. Bcode was invented to provide the same service as uucode but to maintain a tighter standard.

variable width

As applied to a font, variable width means that different characters will have different widths as appropriate. For example, an "i" will take up much less space than an "m". The opposite of variable width is fixed width. The terms "proportional width" and "proportionally spaced" mean the same thing as variable width. Some common variable width fonts include Times, Helvetica, and Bookman.

vector

This term has two common meanings. The first is in the geometric sense: a vector defines a direction and magnitude. The second concerns the formatting of fonts and images. If a font is a vector font or an image is a vector image, it is defined as lines of relative size and direction rather than as collections of pixels (the method used in bitmapped fonts and images). This makes it easier to change the size of the font or image, but puts a bigger load on the device that has to display the font or image. The term "outline font" means the same thing as vector font.

VIC-20
The Commodore VIC-20 computer sold millions of units and is generally considered to have been the first affordable home computer. It features a ROM-based BASIC and uses it as a default "OS". It is based on the 65xx family of processors. VIC (in case you are wondering) can stand for either video interface **c** or video interface computer. The VIC-20 is the precursor to the C64/128.
virtual machine
A virtual machine is a machine completely defined and implemented in software rather than hardware. It is often referred to as a "runtime environment"; code compiled for such a machine is typically called bytecode.
virtual memory
This is a scheme by which disk space is made to substitute for the more expensive RAM space. Using it will often enable a comptuer to do things it could not do without it, but it will also often result in an overall slowing down of the system. The concept of swap space is very similar.
virtual reality
Virtual reality (often called VR for short) is generally speaking an attempt to provide more natural, human interfaces to software. It can be as simple as a pseudo 3D interface or as elaborate as an isolated room in which the computer can control the user's senses of vision, hearing, and even smell and touch.
virus
A virus is a program that will seek to duplicate itself in memory and on disks, but in a subtle way that will not immediately be noticed. A computer on the same network as an infected computer or that uses an infected disk (even a floppy) or that downloads and runs an infected program can itself become infected. A virus can only spread to computers of the same platform. For example, on a network consisting of a WinTel box, a Mac, and a Linux box, if one machine acquires a virus the other two will probably still be safe.
VMS
The industrial strength OS that runs on VAXen.
VoIP
VoIP means "Voice over IP" and it is quite simply a way of utilizing the Internet (or even in some cases intranets) for telephone conversations. The primary motivations for doing so are cost and convenience as VoIP is significantly less expensive than typical telephone long distance packages, plus one high speed Internet connection can serve for multiple phone lines.
VRML
A Virtual Reality Modeling Language file is used to represent VR objects. It has essentially been superceded by X3D.
W3C
The World Wide Web Consortium (usually abbreviated W3C) is a non-profit, advisory body that makes suggestions on the future direction of the World Wide Web, HTML, CSS, and browsers.
Waba
An extremely lightweight subset of Java optimized for use on PDAs.
WebDAV
WebDAV stands for Web-based Distributed Authoring and Versioning, and is designed to provide a way of editing Web-based resources in place. It serves as a more modern (and often more secure) replacement for FTP in many cases.
WebTV
A1NebTV box hooks up to an ordinary television set and displays web pages. It will not display them as well as a dedicated computer.
window manager
A window manager is a program that acts as a graphical go-between for a user and an OS. It provides a GUI for the OS. Some OSes incorporate the window manager into their own internal code, but many do not for reasons of efficiency. Some OSes partially make the division. Some

common true window managers include CDE (Common Desktop Environment), GNOME, KDE, Aqua, OpenWindows, Motif, FVWM, Sugar, and Enlightenment. Some common hybrid window managers with OS extensions include Windows ME, Windows 98, Windows 95, Windows 3.1, OS/2 and GEOS.

WinTel

An x86 based system running some flavor of MS-Windows.

workstation

Depending upon whom you ask, a workstation is either an industrial strength desktop computer or its own category above the desktops. Workstations typically have some flavor of UNIX for their OS, but there has been a recent trend to call high-end Windows NT and Windows 2000 machines workstations, too.

WYSIWYG

What you see is what you get; an adjective applied to a program that attempts to exactly represent printed output on the screen. Related to WYSIWYM but quite different.

WYSIWYM

What you see is what you mean; an adjective applied to a program that does not attempt to exactly represent printed output on the screen, but rather defines how things are used and so will adapt to different paper sizes, etc. Related to WYSIWYG but quite different.

X-Face

X-Faces are small monochrome images embedded in headers for both provides a e-mail and news messages. Better mail and news applications will display them (sometimes automatically, sometimes only per request).

X-Windows

X-Windows provides a GUI for most UNIX systems, but can also be found as an add-on library for other computers. Numerous window managers run on top of it. It is often just called "X".

X3D

Extensible **3D** Graphics data is an XML file that is used to hold three-dimensional graphical data. It is the successor to VRML.

x86

The x86 series of processors includes the Pentium, Pentium Pro, Pentium II, Pentium III, Celeron, and Athlon as well as the 786, 686, 586, 486, 386, 286, 8086, 8088, etc. It is an exceptionally popular design (by far the most popular CISC series) in spite of the fact that even its fastest model is significantly slower than the assorted RISC processors. Many different OSes run on machines built around x86 processors, including MS-DOS, Windows 3.1, Windows '95, Windows '98, Windows ME, Windows NT, Windows 2000, Windows CE, Windows XP, GEOS, Linux, Solaris, OpenBSD, NetBSD, FreeBSD, Mac OS X, OS/2, BeOS, CP/M, etc. A couple different companies produce x86 processors, but the bulk of them are produced by Intel. It is expected that this processor will eventually be completely replaced by the Merced, but the Merced development schedule is somewhat behind. Also, it should be noted that the Pentium III processor has stirred some controversy by including a "fingerprint" that will enable individual computer usage of web pages etc. to be accurately tracked.

XBL

An XML Binding Language document is used to associate executable content with an XML tag. It is itself an XML file, and is used most frequently (although not exclusively) in conjunction with XUL.

XHTML

The Extensible Hypertext Mark-up Language is essentially a cleaner, stricter version of HTML. It is a proper subset of XML.

XML

The Extensible Mark-up Language is a subset of SGML and a superset of XHTML. It is used for numerous things including (among many others) RSS and RDF.

XML-RPC
XML-RPC provides a fairly lightweight means by which one computer can execute a program on a co-operating machine across a network like the Internet. It is based on XML and is used for everything from fetching stock quotes to checking weather forcasts.
XO
The energy-efficient, kid-friendly laptop produced by the OLPC project. It runs Sugar for its window manager and Linux for its OS. It sports numerous built-in features like wireless networking, a video camera & microphone, a few USB ports, and audio in/out jacks. It comes with several educational applications (which it refers to as "Activities"), most of which are written in Python.
XSL
The Extensible Stylesheet Language is like CSS for XML. It provides a means of describing how an XML resource should be displayed.
XSLT
XSL Transformations are used to transform one type of XML into another. It is a component of XSL that can be (and often is) used independently.
XUL
An XML User-Interface Language document is used to define a user interface for an application using XML to specify the individual controls as well as the overall layout.
Z-Machine
A virtual machine optimized for running interactive fiction, interactive tutorials, and other interactive things of a primarily textual nature. Z-Machines have been ported to almost every platform in use today. Z-machine bytecode is usually called Z-code. The Glulx virtual machine is of the same idea but somewhat more modern in concept.
zip
There are three common zips in the computer world that are completely different from one another. One is a type of removable removable disk slightly larger (physically) and vastly larger (capacity) than a floppy. The second is a group of programs used for running interactive fiction. The third is a group of programs used for compression.

www.ingramcontent.com/pod-product-compliance
Lightning Source LLC
Chambersburg PA
CBHW082208300426

44117CB00016B/2714